You're Not Dead Yet!
How to Live Well, Laugh Often and Graduate Life with Honors

Kathy Dempsey
Kim Harms

Copyright © 2025 Kathy Dempsey & Kim Harms

Shed or You're Dead, Lenny the Lizard, and SHED® logo
are trademarks of Kathy Dempsey

All rights reserved.
No part of this book may be used or reproduced in any manner whatsoever without the written permission of the authors, except in the case of brief quotations embodied in reviews and certain other non-commercial uses permitted by copyright law.

Published by Trey Press
Phoenix, Arizona

Cover Layout: Singles Design

ISBN: 979-8-9993528-0-4

You're Not Dead Yet!
How to Live Well, Laugh Often and Graduate Life with Honors

Kathy Dempsey
Kim Harms

Table of Contents

Foreword:
Why I wrote this book Kathy Dempsey 1
Why I wrote this book Kim Harms 7

Introduction: 13
The Many Faces of Death: Embracing the Inevitable
    with Purpose 14

**Part 1: Shedding: A Lifelong Journey from First Breath
to Final Bow—Mastering the Art of Living Well** 19
The Philosophy of Shedding 20
The Process of Shedding 20
Rapid Shedding: The Antidote to the Change Crisis 21
Your First Shedding Experience 22
SHED HAPPENS: It's Part of Life 24
SHED HAPPENS Inventory 25
Kathy's Unexpected Death Sentence at 25 29
The 3 R's of Shedding 33
The Shedding Revolution's 5 Stages of Change 35
Overcoming Fear: The Biggest Barrier to Shedding 39
SHED Management 42
    Control Management 42
    Energy Management 45
    Be in the NOW Management 56
The Big Three: Shedding Roles, Stuff & Stories 58
Shedding Expectations 62
Helping Kids SHED 63

Part 2: More Life Skills for Living Well .69
Grappling with Grief 70
Managing Conflict and the Art of Peacemaking 77
I Can Do it Myself...Until I Can't 83
How to Get Along with Your Adult Children Without
    Really Trying (and Vice Versa) 91

Conquering Loneliness 97
Bend Don't Break: The Power of Resilience 101
Laughing Through the Aches: A Seniors Guide to Growing Old .105
Success and Retirement: Finding Your Purpose 112
Escape from the Valley of the Scammed .119
They Didn't Just Steal My Data, They Highjacked My Life 126

Part 3: Taking Care of YOU 131
Take Care of Yourself - Physically 132
Take Care of Yourself - Mentally 135
Take Care of Yourself - Spiritually 136
Take Care of Yourself - Financially 137

Part 4: Dying Well — A Graceful Exit that Prevents Chaos, Ends Conflict, and Secures Your Legacy 141
Dying Well: The Final Act of Living Well 142
What is Your Legacy: Building Emotional Wealth for
 Your Loved Ones 147
Closing Thoughts: Your Invitation to Start Now 152

**BONUS: RethinkingDeath.Life WORKBOOK –
ONE BINDER TO RULE THEM ALL** 155
An Important Workbook to Spare Your Family Pain and
 Provide Your Family Peace 157
Death Preppers Goal-Setting Guide 160
The Grateful But Not Yet Dead Tour: Why Wait for the
 Funeral to Tell People You Love Them 164
The Exit Interview You Need to Plan Now 167
Your Last Will & Testament: Where Do All Your Valuables Go? .170
Letter of Intent/Instruction 173
Getting Rid of Your Other Stuff 176
Healthcare Directives 178
Organ Donation 181
Do You Want a Party or Living Wake? 183
Living Funerals (Kathy) 185

Table of Contents

Writing Your Obituary 190
Selecting Your Obituary and Memorial Service Pictures 194
Where Will My Remains Remain? 196
What Do You Want On Your Tombstone? 199
Funeral Planning: Acknowledging Your Appointment
    With Death 201
Documenting Your Family History 203
Legacy Letters and Legacy Love Letters 209
Reconciliation Letters 215
Apology Letters 218
Living Well & Dying Well Question prompts 221
Bio Kimberly Harms 223
Bio Kathy B. Dempsey 226
Bio Lenny T. Lizard 229
How Can We Help? Services 230

You're Not Dead Yet!

Forward

KATHY DEMPSEY
Why I Wrote This Book.

You die well by living well today.
—Ron Black

I met Ron on Match.com. And from our very first conversation, there was a spark that lit up everything. It wasn't just chemistry—it was connection. We both loved adventure, the outdoors, working out, and soaking up every ounce of life. And we laughed—constantly. We would lose track of time talking and laughing for hours. Ron had an incredible sense of humor, quick, playful, a bit sarcastic (he was born in the Bronx), and full of heart. I would often look at him and think, *Is this real?* Life couldn't have been better. I would literally pinch myself.

One Saturday morning, we woke up with that lightness in our hearts that comes from looking forward to something big. We had just booked our long-awaited trip to Maui—tickets and condo, done. We were dancing around the house, celebrating, and playing the iconic ukulele-backed rendition of "Somewhere Over the Rainbow" by Israel "IZ" Kamakawiwo'ole. The whole morning felt like a dream.

Then we hopped on our bikes for our usual 15-mile loop around the lake. Halfway through the ride, Ron's phone rang. He stopped, looked at the screen, and casually said, "I'll call him back later."

"Who was it?" I asked. "My doctor," he replied. "Just a routine follow-up. I had a physical last week. I feel great—nothing's wrong."

But my ER nurse instincts kicked in fast.

"Doctors don't call you at 8 a.m. on a Saturday unless something's wrong," I said. "Call him back, NOW." He did.

I could hear the urgency in the doctor's voice even from across the bike path: "You need to get to the emergency room immediately. Your potassium is at a panic level. I've never seen anyone walking around alive with it this high. You should be dead."

Ron looked at me, stunned. After some convincing, we turned around and pedaled straight to the hospital. At the ER, lab tests confirmed the numbers were real. The team rushed in—IVs, medications, EKG, scans. Chaos in motion. Hours later, the doctor came back into the room with a different kind of quiet. The kind that makes your stomach drop before a word is even spoken.

"I'm so sorry," he said. "You have stage 4 renal cancer." My heart stopped. I knew in that moment—life would never be the same again.

But here's what we did next: We didn't spiral. We didn't retreat.

We made two clear commitments—sacred, simple, and strong:
1. We would walk the journey together.
2. And we would bring as much JOY to each situation as possible.

We adjusted and readjusted. Plans changed. Dreams rerouted. We canceled our long-awaited trip to Hawaii and had a virtual island escape right here in the Arizona desert—steel drum music, fruity drinks, and the two of us pretending we were on the beach—choosing joy even when the future was uncertain.

Through every up and down, every curveball life threw, Ron was ready. Every challenge was met with Ron's trademark response: bounce back fast, crack a joke, and keep going—shielded by that invisible armor of humor and hope.

Forward

I'll never forget our Valentine's Day. It wasn't candlelit. It was spent under fluorescent lights in the oncologist's office. We sat side by side, holding hands, bracing ourselves. The doctor walked in, holding a clipboard like a shield. He didn't look up. In a voice void of emotion—more machine than man—he said: "The pathology report is back. The cancer has spread to the lungs, the pancreas, the liver, the bones…"

Before he could finish, I blurted out, "What's the good news?" It just slipped out—part reflex, part prayer. He paused. Finally met my eyes. "It hasn't hit the brain."

Walking out of the doctor's office, Ron, ever the comedian, gave me a smirk and said, "Well… I guess I don't have to worry about retirement anymore."

That was classic Ron. He'd always said, "If I get bad news, I'm heading straight to the guitar store." And true to his word, that's exactly what we did. We walked into the shop and passed two massive signs: one said GUITARS, the other ORGANS/PIANOS. A salesclerk asked, "Can I help you?" Ron nodded. "Actually, I came in for guitars, but now I see you also sell organs."

"Do you need an organ?" Without missing a beat: "Yeah. A kidney, a pancreas, and a liver—for starters." I rolled my eyes, laughing, and nudged him forward. "He's just a little strung out. Can you point us to the guitars?"

He picked one off the wall, tuned it, and looked at me with a wink. "Kathy, this one's for you." He started strumming "Always Look on the Bright Side of Life." I joined in. Then a few customers. Then the entire store. Even cancer had to wait while Ron played.

But not for long.

A few weeks later, the cancer did hit the brain. Ron had a stroke and was paralyzed on his left side. After looking at the CT scan of the brain with the neuro-oncologist in Mayo Clinic's ICU, it was obvious—this was the final gunshot wound to the brain. I knew it was time.

With tears flowing, I stood at the nurse's station and did the hardest thing I've ever done. I signed the papers to stop dialysis. To let Ron die. It was the right decision. A final act of love…but it felt like my heart had been ripped in two.

Ron was transferred to a hospice facility a few miles away. I climbed into the back of the ambulance and held his hand the entire ride. Through the window, the Arizona mountains stood silent—steadfast witnesses to our journey. We'd driven past them countless times before—on our way to dinners, hikes, celebrations, ordinary days. But this time… it was different. This was our last ride together.

When we arrived, I turned his room into a sanctuary of sound—guitars, a keyboard, his favorite music playing softly through the speakers. I filled the space with love, lavender, and presence.

That evening, I asked him, "Do you need anything?" He looked at me and said, "Yeah. I want an interactive funeral." "Wait—what?" "I want to be alive at my funeral."

Within 24 hours, we made it happen. The community room was filled—standing room only. Friends showed up. Others joined by Skype and phone, and others left messages for Ron to be read from around the world. There were guitars, banjos, keyboards, and laughter. There was music and memory and Ron—leading it all from his wheelchair, air guitar in full swing.

He had us laughing one minute and crying the next. When the nurses wheeled him back to his room, I leaned in and asked: "Ron, how are you doing this? How are you dying so well? I did my master's thesis on death & dying. Teach me."

Forward

He looked at me, calm and steady. "You die well by living well today." That sentence settled into my bones. It wasn't just an answer—it was a truth. One that would echo in me for the rest of my life.

And then... something unexpected happened. The next morning, I looked in the mirror—eyes puffy, heart full—and said out loud, almost in disbelief: "You're getting married today." I pulled out my parents' wedding rings from my jewelry box, tucked them into my pocket, and hopped on my bike and made my way back to the hospice.

We had never talked about marriage. Not once. My stomach twisted with nerves. Mouth dry. What if he says no? What if a dying man tells you no? That'll be ten more years of therapy.

I walked in, kissed his forehead and said, "Good morning, Sweetheart." He turned to me slowly, his eyes still full of light. "I have a question to ask you," I said. I took a deep breath. "Will you marry me?"

There was a long pause. And then, with a whisper and the faintest smile, he said: "Yeeeeesssss..." I jumped up, hands in the air, laughing through tears.

Moments later, there was a knock at the door—it was the hospice chaplain. "Can I help you?" I grinned. "Do you marry people?" He smiled back. "I do. My wedding book is in the car—I'll go get it."

And just like that, we got married. Right there, bedside. The chaplain sat on the edge of the bed and performed the ceremony. Friends came with cake and cards. Someone brought flowers. We toasted with the bottle of water Ron had saved from our very first date—because some things, you just don't SHED.

I thanked him for five amazing years. And he looked at me and said: "And the next five are going to be even more amazing."

That was the last day Ron was conscious. Three days later, he passed.

But before he left, he gave me the greatest gift: a roadmap, a mantra, a way to live with intention and without regret.

"You die well by living well today."

After Ron died, I was devastated. The grief was raw, deep, and at times unbearable. I knew I couldn't just push through it—I needed to truly heal. So, I stepped away from everything and took a three-month sabbatical. I moved into a quiet cabin in Sedona, nestled by a babbling creek, surrounded by red rocks and silence. I even took care of two sheep—gentle, grounding companions during a time when I felt anything but steady.

That time was sacred. It allowed me to begin healing not just physically, but mentally and spiritually. In the stillness, in the care of simple creatures, and in the heart of nature, I began to rediscover what it means to live well... even in the face of loss.

So, here's the good news: **You're Not Dead Yet**. That means you still have time. Time to SHED what no longer serves you. Time to rewrite your story, love more freely, laugh more loudly, and live like you mean it.

This isn't a book about endings—it's about beginnings. It's about waking up to what really matters, while you still have breath to give and love to share. If you listen closely, you might even hear Ron whispering from beyond: **"You die well by living well today."**

So, let's get started. It's time to **rethink everything you thought you knew about death—and about life**.

For Ron—
Who taught me how to Live Well. Die Well.

Kathy Dempsey

Forward

KIM HARMS
Why I Wrote This Book.

I didn't plan to write a book about learning to live fully before dying. But then again, I didn't plan to lose a child, a husband, and my career either. Life—and death—had other ideas.

A happy life, a sad life, a traumatic life—these are all relative terms. Just ask my friends in Rwanda, where joy is pursued not in the absence of pain, but in defiance of it. My contribution to this book is built on two things: the lessons life has carved into me and the credentials I've earned along the way. My deepest hope is that the guidance in these pages will help us all live more fully now—and ensure that those we love will grieve with less pain and grow with more peace when we're gone.

My life began with loss. I was born with only 7 fingers and spinal abnormalities. When I was three my parents divorced. My brother, sister and I lived with our beautiful, kind, loving and compassionate mother and equally loving grandmother. Life was good.

My father remarried but forgot to tell his new wife that he had three children. Oops!

At 6 my father discovered that a drug that my mother had taken for morning sickness and which was being tested in Cincinnati, Thalidomide, was the likely culprit for my missing fingers. He promptly informed mom of this news. She was devastated by guilt. That guilt triggered a short hospitalization for mental illness. Her hospitalization triggered her children being taken away from her. My father would not return us when she was released, and she never recovered. Mom died by suicide in that mental health hospital when I was 17.

Life with my father and stepmother (who had never signed up to take care of three children) was miserable. All three of us escaped as soon as we could. Fortunately, I chose a healthy escape, college. I worked three jobs to pay tuition.

Those two major losses of my mother—first to an institution and then to suicide, left permanent scars that shape my life to this day. And yet, the love and support that I got for those first 6 years from my mother and grandmother carried me through the dark times and gave me the quiet determination to pass those same virtues on to my children and grandchildren.

In college, I met a wonderful man who wanted to be a dentist. His name was Jim Harms. I decided that maybe, if I became a dentist too and had a good job, he would marry me. Please don't judge me. This was the 70's after all. At that time, women were becoming liberated from such thought. Obviously, I was not quite liberated yet.

Anyway, my plan worked, Jim and I were married. We went to dental school together, started a practice in Farmington MN, and had three beautiful children. Life was good again.

But life doesn't let you stay on top of the mountain forever.

In the fall of 2007, my brother Mike died of a heart attack, three months later my husband Jim was diagnosed with liver cancer and a 5% survival rate. Six months after that, Jim was saved with a liver transplant. We celebrated, but only temporarily. In another 6 months our world would explode.

On January 31, 2009, our only son Eric, just 19 years old, died from suicide, just like my mother. He was a freshman at Columbia University in New York.

Eric was an amazing young man. He had a beautiful heart, he was thoughtful, kind and always looked for the person who needed help. He had a brilliant mind, he was a National Merit Scholar, and was elected to student government at Columbia. He was a gifted jazz pianist. When Eric came home for Christmas, his freshman year, he was on top of the world. He had made the Dean's List in engineering and was playing with their jazz program in New York City. Two weeks after returning to his beloved Columbia and just 45 minutes after a breakup with his girlfriend he was gone.

Eric, like too many young people, was the victim of suicidal depression, a natural impulsivity that made him such a good musician and a brain that was not yet fully developed in managing emotional turmoil.

When Eric died, I felt as if my heart had splintered into a million pieces. I couldn't eat, I couldn't sleep, I couldn't' think, and I felt for a while as if I couldn't continue. Each morning, I opened my eyes hoping it had all been a bad dream—only to be crushed by the truth that it wasn't. This was real. And it wasn't going away. Everything I once enjoyed became either painful or pointless. Books sat unopened, hobbies abandoned, and I avoided anything involving conflict or pain.

I felt as if a big fishing net was strangling my heart and pulling me under. Emotionally I was drowning. I went to work but I resigned from all of my outside activities.

A few months after Eric died, I was given an extraordinary gift. I was leaving my dental office, and in that zombie stage of grief, dead on the inside and trying to look alive on the outside, when I was approached angrily by Jim's cousin. He wagged his finger in my face and with anger in his voice said, *"Don't you ever make your remaining children feel that they are not enough. Don't you do that to them!"*

His words hit me like a lightning bolt. He had lost his brother at about the same age as Eric, and he felt that he lost his parents at the same time. He believed that his parents were so consumed with grief over their dead son, that they were not able to attend to the needs of their living children. And I was headed down that same path. I loved my family and wouldn't dream of doing anything that would cause them more pain. At that moment I became determined to fight, kick and scream my way out of that grief pit, for my family and for myself.

Escaping grief is not easy, it never is. It takes time and it takes determination. But being able to breathe again and live in the moment is totally worth the effort.

One year later, I was diagnosed with permanent nerve damage to my drilling fingers and my clinical career in dentistry was over in one day. I asked God, "Really! Haven't I suffered enough? Why me?" At the same time, however, I realized that losing my career wasn't the worst thing that had happened to me. Losing Eric put everything into perspective.

In 2020 the loss of our son was compounded by the loss of my husband, Jim, to congestive heart failure and the beginning of my journey through widowhood. I found myself staring at the grief pit again. This time, I was in a new, uncharted place: the dark valley between menopause and death. No roadmap. No guide. Just me, trying to figure out what comes next.

Then it hit me: I'm still here. If I'm still here, then I still have purpose. And my purpose, I discovered, is to live with my legacy in mind and to prepare my family to thrive without me.

Because here's the truth: everything I've been through—every loss, every battle—is useless unless I pass on what I've learned.

So, I became a grief counselor, a death doula, a civil mediator and a life coach. I have written a few books on legacy building and

Forward

widowhood, and I am thrilled to co-write You're Not Dead Yet with the incredible shedding expert Kathy Dempsey.

Together, we explore the truth that to grow into each new chapter of life, we must SHED the old one, like a lizard releasing a too-tight skin or a tree surrendering its fall leaves to make way for spring. From child to student, student to adult, adult to partner, partner to parent, parent to caregiver, caregiver to griever, we are constantly being asked to let go of who we were in order to become who we're meant to be next.

As an older adult, I have already shed the big house and most of my stuff. I have adjusted my relationships with my children, grandchildren, and friends as we all age. I am planning for the next steps in case I become infirm. Life is changing too quickly for my taste, but change will continue whether I like it or not. My job is to get ready for the next step, adjust, and to realize that my legacy isn't in the stuff, it is in the love and lessons I leave behind.

My goal is that after reading this book, you'll feel more confident about how to live well now and leave an extraordinary emotional legacy for your family. Take time to organize your affairs to ease their burden after your death, have open conversations about death before it happens, and strengthen your relationships through forgiveness, reconciliation, and heartfelt messages of love.

Death comes unexpectedly. Don't assume you have time. Live well now, but prepare for the future. The greatest gift we can give the next generation is not a perfect life, but the tools to weather an imperfect one.

The clock is ticking, the time to get ready is now.

Kim Harms

Kim Harms

You're Not Dead Yet!

Introduction

KIM HARMS

The Many Faces of Death: Embracing the Inevitable with Purpose

Every man dies, but not every man truly lives.
—William Wallace (Braveheart, the movie)

Before we talk about the final breath, we have to talk about all the little deaths that come before it. The death of a dream you once clung to. The slow unraveling of a marriage. The moment a job —or an identity—you built your life around vanishes. The shattering of expectations, the silence after a friendship fades, the ache of letting go of who you thought you'd be. Death comes in many forms, and each one demands a grieving, a reckoning, a rebirth. This book isn't just about dying well—it's about surviving all the deaths we live through before our hearts stop beating.

That being said, our hearts *will* stop beating some day. None of us are getting out of this alive. So why do we act like death is some awkward guest we can ignore forever? Talking about our own death might feel uncomfortable, but not talking about it is like tossing your family a live grenade and yelling, 'Good luck!

So let's pause, take a breath, and face what we've spent a lifetime avoiding.

It's time. You knew this was coming! We put the word "dead" right in the title. Now, we're going to talk about death—not in some vague, abstract way, but about our own death. There, I said it. It's out there now. No turning back. Take a deep breath. We can do this together.

If there's one thing, we all have in common, it's that we are going to die. Hopefully not today, not tomorrow, but someday. And yet, most of us spend our lives pretending that day will never come. We plan for college, careers, and retirement. But how often do we truly prepare for the one certainty in life? I am now in that inescapable phase of life between menopause and death, where my job as a responsible human is to deal with the first and prepare for the second. And honestly, it's freeing. You're Not Dead Yet—so stop running from death and start living like you mean it.

The Price of Avoidance

Most phases of life follow a predictable pattern, but death doesn't play by those rules. It can come suddenly or slowly, expected or unexpected. The only rational response is to prepare—not out of fear, but out of love. Love for the people we leave behind. Love for the legacy we want to leave. Had I started my legacy planning earlier, I wouldn't have a garage packed with things no one wants or a box full of disorganized financial records. I might have used my resources more wisely, invested more in relationships, and worried less about trivial things.

There's a word for the fear of death: thanatophobia. Some fear the process of dying, others fear what comes after. Many of us avoid the topic entirely, hoping that if we don't think about it, it won't happen. But avoidance has consequences. It leaves families in chaos, struggling to untangle financial messes, questioning what their loved one would have wanted, and wrestling with grief on top of stress. I've seen it firsthand. My husband Jim was dying long before anyone said it out loud. No doctor ever told us. But the home health nurses knew. They lovingly intervened and recommended hospice, allowing Jim to die the way he wanted—on his own terms, with dignity, and surrounded by love.

A Call to Prepare

My hope is that this chapter helps you prepare for death—whenever it comes—so that your loved ones aren't left grieving not just your absence, but the disorder left behind. If you feel overwhelmed, you're not alone. According to AARP, 60% of American adults over eighteen don't have a will. The good news? The older we get, the more we understand the importance of taking that first step.

Of course, the best way to extend our years and make the most of them is to care for our health—exercise, eat well, and avoid bad habits. But no matter how many marathons we run or how clean our diet is, death will catch up with us eventually. And when it does, we need a plan.

Where Do You Want to Die?
More and more people are choosing to die at home. According to the New England Journal of Medicine, in 2017, 30.7% of Americans died at home, surpassing hospital deaths (29.8%) for the first time in over a century. Hospice deaths are increasing, while nursing home deaths are declining. This shift shows that people want comfort and familiarity in their final moments. But for that to happen, we must have conversations—about what we want, where we want to be, and who we want by our side.

The Role of a Death Doula
In preparing for this book, I became certified as a death doula—someone trained to provide emotional and spiritual care at the end of life. My co-author and dear friend Kathy also became a death doula. We are not acting as medical professionals, but we walk alongside the dying and their families, listening, supporting, and honoring their wishes. One of the greatest examples of a death doula was Mother Teresa. She devoted her life to caring for the dying, believing that every person deserved to die with dignity and love.

One of the most sacred roles of a death doula is simply listening. Sometimes, the dying need permission to let go. Other times, they need someone to help them create a legacy—whether through letters, videos, or shared memories. And yes, sometimes we just hold space, sitting in the quiet with them, bearing witness to their final moments.

Even those who seem unconscious may still hear us. That's why it's important to speak with love and reassurance. Tell them they are loved. Tell them they can go in peace. It's a gift to be fully present in someone's last moments—a privilege, really.

Introduction

Living Well to Die Well
An important question to ask anyone facing death is: How do you want to live today? The best reason to get your affairs in order is so that when your time comes, you can focus on living, not worrying.

When Jim was dying, I was grateful that we had everything in place—hospice care, an adjustable bed, oxygen, a single-story home that made things easier. His sisters, Judy and Sue, were always there, stepping in as unofficial death doulas. I will always be thankful for them. Death isn't something we're meant to navigate alone.

The Power of Legacy
Of all the roles of a death doula, my favorite is helping people create legacy projects. A legacy is more than money or possessions; it's the stories we leave behind, the wisdom we pass on, the love we share.

One of the first legacy projects I worked on was with my son, Eric. In high school, he and I transcribed and digitized the diary of a World War II tail gunner turned dentist. His words transported us to another time—a time of bravery, loss, and deep camaraderie. One entry haunts me still. He had been wounded and sent to the hospital. The next day, his plane took off without him and was shot down. Every member of his crew was lost. He carried the weight of that survivor's guilt for the rest of his life.

Death doesn't always make sense. It doesn't follow rules. But stories like his remind us why our lives matter—why the legacy we leave is so important. If we are still here, we still have a purpose.

Final Thoughts
We don't get to choose when we die. But we do get to choose how we live. And we get to choose how we prepare. Let's stop avoiding the conversation. Let's embrace it. Not with fear, but with purpose. Because in the end, a well-lived life is the best preparation for a peaceful death.

Are you ready?

PART 1
SHEDDING:

A LIFELONG JOURNEY FROM FIRST BREATH TO FINAL BOW— MASTERING THE ART OF LIVING WELL

KATHY DEMPSEY

The Philosophy of Shedding

On July 29, 1998, at a hospital ethics meeting, I bumped into a colleague, David Mann. When I asked how he was, he replied, "Fine, but my lizard is dead." It died because it couldn't shed its skin. "Lizards grow by shedding," he said. "No shedding, no growth. No growth, death."

That moment sparked a powerful realization: humans must shed too—old habits, toxic thoughts, toxic relationships—to grow. That day, **Shed or You're Dead**® was born, along with **Lenny the Lizard**, my longtime metaphorical mentor.

So, what about you? What do you need to shed to grow into who you're meant to be?

The Process of Shedding
Shedding is a two-part process:

Letting go of the old.
1. "The old" includes anything that's no longer healthy, helpful, or relevant. It might have served you once—but not anymore.

    Remember corded phones? At one time, they were essential. You couldn't imagine life without one. But now, we carry smartphones in our pockets with far more capability and freedom. The corded phone wasn't bad, you just outgrew it.

Taking on the new.
2. The second part of shedding is embracing new skills, fresh mindsets, and healthier habits that help you grow into who you're becoming.

You can't move forward while holding on to what's holding you back.

Part 1: Shedding

The Continuous Cycle of Shedding

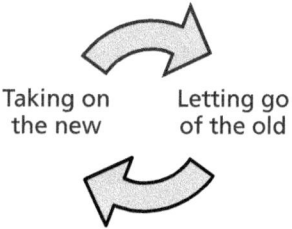

Taking on the new   Letting go of the old

» Routinely ask yourself, what no longer serves me? «

Rapid Shedding: The Antidote to the Change Crisis

We're not just experiencing change—we're living in a full-blown **change crisis**. Experts say you'll face more change this year than your grandparents did in their entire lives.

In the past, change came in waves—intense, then calm. Like tides. Predictable.

The Change Crisis: How change is changing

Today, change is a never-ending tidal wave. No breaks. No breathers. Just more.

That's why shedding isn't optional, it's essential.

To survive this pace, we need to master *rapid shedding*—the ability to quickly let go of what no longer serves us and adapt in real-time. It's not about keeping up anymore. It's about staying *ready*. Buckle up—this wave isn't slowing down.

Shedding Rules
1. Everything is changing
2. Suffering occurs when humans try to hold on to what is changing
3. The key to life is embracing certain uncertainty

Lenny's college professor at Reptile University

Your First Shedding Experience

The basis of shedding, or change, is rooted in two of life's core necessities: **attachment and detachment**.

Do you remember being born? If not, take your hand and feel the button in the middle of your stomach. It's evidence you were there! Imagine you are back in your mom's womb. It was warm and secure.

You didn't have to worry about paying the rent or mortgage. You had a nine-month rent free lease! You didn't have to worry about going to the grocery store or the kids yelling, *"What are we going to have for dinner?"* You had a 24/7 infusion of nutrition.

You didn't have to worry about bills, or bosses, or teenagers, or anyone. Your biggest job was just floating and freeloading. Life was good.

What happened nine months later? You were evicted! Mom decided to downsize! Fetal foreclosure! Then what did somebody do with a pair of scissors? They cut the cord.

And how did we respond? We cried! Loudly! If we could've talked, we might've screamed: *Where am I going to live? What am I going to eat?*

Part 1: Shedding

Why did you cut off my food supply?! It's cold out here! And let's be honest—most of us would've said: **Put me back in!**

From the day you were born until the day you die; you will continually go through a series of attachments and detachments. Not physical ones like being attached to your mom by a cord, but emotional ones. Your ability to deal with life's attachments is critical for your success and happiness. The primary focus of attachments at birth (our cord) and at death (our bodies) are physical. However, the primary focus of attachments throughout the rest of our lives are emotional.

Primary Focus of Attachments

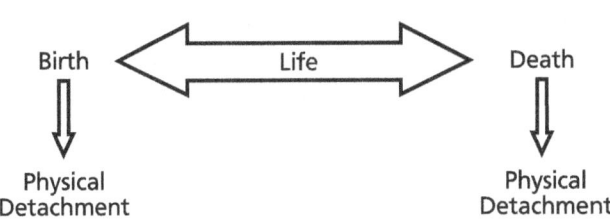

Life then becomes a series of shedding: identities, relationships, routines, roles... even dreams. We grow by letting go.

Change = Loss. Loss = Grief.
"And grief? It's not just sadness. It's a process: **Denial, Anger, Bargaining, Depression, Acceptance**," as Elisabeth Kübler-Ross, the pioneer in the field of death and dying, taught us.

If shedding is something we all face—from cradle to grave—shouldn't we know how to do it well? The truth is none of us got a manual. There was no "Shedding 101" in school. Instead, we learned by watching the people around us; parents, teachers, and friends, many of whom were just trying to survive their own shedding seasons, often without the tools themselves.

Shedding well *is* living well—no matter where you are on the journey. And the beautiful thing is... **you're not dead yet**. Which means there's still time to learn the art of letting go and growing forward. It's a skill. And like any skill, it starts right here. Right now.

LENNY'S WISDOM:

They didn't teach shedding in school. But they should've—right after taxes and how to survive a hot flash in Spanx. Midlife isn't a crisis. It's a clearance sale. SHED what's not serving you anymore and make room for joy.

SHED HAPPENS: It's Part of Life.

Most of us want to live happy and carefree lives, but none of us ever do. Instead, we experience obstacles, challenges, and problems. From birth to death, life is full of unpredictable and unexpected challenges, some of which we have no control over, some of which we have some control over. Regardless, we all know when SHED HAPPENS.

Part 1: Shedding

SHED HAPPENS Inventory

Take a few minutes and review the following examples of SHED HAPPENS. Circle the ones that have happened to you.

1. Death of a spouse
2. Divorce
3. Relationship breakup
4. Diagnosis of life-threatening disease
5. Death of a child
6. Death of family member
7. Death of close friend
8. Unplanned pregnancy
9. Marital difficulties
10. Getting fired
11. Financial difficulties
12. Personal injury
13. Arrested by police
14. Death of pet
15. Being falsely accused of something you didn't do
16. Foreclosure on mortgage or loan
17. Bankruptcy
18. Problems with in-laws
19. Management issues with boss or company
20. Merger or acquisition of your company
21. Job elimination
22. Job transfer and relocation
23. Motor vehicle accident
24. Flat tire
25. Cell phone breaks or is lost
26. Insomnia
27. Hospitalization
28. Family member/friend with mental illness or addiction issues
29. Speeding/parking ticket
30. Partner is late for dinner/event
31. Getting lost

32. Failing a test
33. Health challenge
34. Being lied to
35. Infidelity
36. Family member/friend diagnosed with illness
37. Adult children making unhealthy choices
38. Work demands to do more with less
39. Unmanageable weight issues
40. Being left on hold on phone for customer service issues
41. Inability to get a live person on the phone
42. Being late for meeting or event
43. Children getting into trouble at school
44. Being cut off while driving
45. Someone not paying you back
46. Someone lying to you
47. Someone not keeping their promise
48. Forced retirement
49. Acquiring a visible deformity
50. Natural weather disasters
51. Being a victim of a crime
52. Unexpected work challenges
53. Chronic pain
54. Getting older and loss of independence
55. Being treated disrespectfully
56. Someone not acknowledging your feelings
57. Surgery
58. Air flight is delayed or cancelled
59. Getting lost
60. Losing something of value
61. Not being heard
62. Forgetting your computer passwords
63. Feeling underappreciated
64. Technology fails
65. Anxiety
66. Depression

67. Suicide of family member or close friend
68. Estranged from family member or close friend
69. Physical and/or emotional abuse
70. Multiple deaths or losses in a short amount of time.
71. Loss of a business or major client
72. Identity theft or financial fraud
73. Difficulty conceiving a child or infertility
74. Becoming responsible as a caregiver for an aging parent
75. Being publicly humiliated or shamed (online or in-person)
76. Loss of a close friendship due to conflict or drifting apart
77. Cultural or racial discrimination
78. Experiencing a miscarriage
79. Legal battles (lawsuits, custody disputes, etc.)
80. Global Pandemic
    And you can add more of your own.

How many did you have? _____

Life is always going to present us with problems and obstacles. Yet, problems can become opportunities for growth.

It's not what happens to you in life; it's how you respond to it.
—Victor Frankl

When SHED HAPPENS… Don't Get Stuck in the Why Me?
After the shock of shedding—the job loss, the diagnosis, the divorce, the disappointment—it's human to ask: *Why* is this happening to me?

Asking this question is the anthem of the victim mindset. And while it's a completely valid *emotional* response, staying there keeps you stuck. But what if you turned that question on its head?

What if life isn't happening **to** you… but **for** you?

What if this unwanted change is actually a custom-designed invitation to grow, heal, release, or realign? Pain has a purpose. It's not punishment. It's not karma keeping score. It's often the clearest messenger that something needs to be SHED—even when you didn't choose it.

So instead of getting trapped in victim mode, try asking:
- What is life trying to teach me through this?
- What am I being called to release or outgrow?
- Where might this be guiding me back to my true self?

You're not powerless. You're in a shedding season. And like all seasons—it will pass. But who you become because of it? That's up to you.

*Life is not happening **to** you, but **for** you.* —Kathy Dempsey

The Gift in the Grief

Grief doesn't just show up when someone dies. It arrives when anything ends—relationships, roles, routines, health, homes, hopes. When grief knocks, it often feels like something has been ripped away. And it has.

But if you sit with it—*really* sit with it. Grief can become a sacred teacher.

Grief slows us down. It strips away the nonessential. It reveals what matters most. It doesn't come to destroy you. It comes to **reshape you**. Yes, it hurts. Yes, it's messy. But hidden inside grief is a gift: A deeper capacity to feel, to love, to empathize. A renewed sense of what's meaningful. A wake-up call to live more intentionally.

We don't SHED without some form of grief. But when you allow the tears to water your soul, something unexpected grows. **Clarity. Compassion. Courage. Connection.**

So don't rush your grief. Don't numb it or bypass it. Hold it gently. Listen closely.

Part 1: Shedding

Because underneath the ache, there's wisdom. And maybe—even beauty.

LENNY'S WISDOM:

I once thought shedding my tail was the worst thing that ever happened to me. Turns out, it grew back stronger—and so did I. Grief feels like loss, but sometimes it's just life making room for what's next. Hang in there, something beautiful is growing beneath the ache.

Kathy's Unexpected Death Sentence at 25 (My Shed Happens Story)

They told me I was going to die.

My ears burned as Dr. Gazaleh blurted out, "Kathy, your AIDS test... it's come back positive." That Wednesday afternoon is a moment I will never forget.

As I hung up the phone, a tremor began in my hands and swept through my body like a shock wave. I was a nurse, just 25 years old, working in the ER trauma unit in June 1986 when a young accident victim was rushed in. We cracked open his chest to perform internal CPR. My hands were wrist-deep inside him. Despite our best efforts, he died. Later that night, we got the news: he had AIDS.

Believe it or not, back then we didn't wear gloves to protect ourselves. I looked down at a small cut on my right index finger and froze. Because of that exposure, I was tested every three months for a year. The first three tests were negative. I thought I was safe. I was wrong.

After that dreadful call, I rushed to the hospital to meet with the doctors. My head was spinning. My hands shook as I gripped the steering wheel. I kept thinking, *This can't be happening. Why me? I was just trying to help someone. I wasn't ready to die. My life was just starting.* The doctors ran additional tests to confirm the diagnosis. Two weeks later, the results came back positive again. The Centers for Disease Control (CDC) was notified.

Why? **Because I was the first healthcare worker in America to test positive for HIV from an on-the-job exposure.** At that time, AIDS was a death sentence. No treatment. No cure. No clear understanding of how it spread. Just fear and stigma. I wasn't just afraid of dying—I was afraid of becoming the poster child for the CDC.

That night, I sat down and told my family. My parents and my sister Virginia stood by me without hesitation. Their love didn't waver.

Days later, I reluctantly told my boss. She was sympathetic, but her words still haunt me: "Kathy, if this news gets out, the hospital will shut down. I'm sorry, but you can't work here anymore." I lost my job.

That weekend, I shared the news with my church. I expected support. Instead, I saw backs turn. People whispered that AIDS was a punishment. The fact that I had contracted it trying to save a life didn't seem to matter. Even some of my closest friends pulled away. Fear replaced friendship. I stopped eating. I stopped sleeping. I was unraveling.

My lowest point was one night, during graduate school, my professor announced we'd be watching a documentary: *Living with AIDS.* As I sat in class, my chest tight and my head spinning, I watched young people—my age—waste away on the screen. My classmates spoke in horror about the disease. They had no idea I was living the nightmare.

Walking out of the classroom, I knew one thing for certain: I wouldn't waste away. I wouldn't die slowly, riddled with suffering and shame. I couldn't. I wouldn't. I decided: **I will choose how I die.**

I got in my car, and I drove aimlessly until I found myself in the parking lot of Chattanooga's most well-known hotel. My thoughts raced, looping around a track called *regrets*. I regretted not spending more time with my family and friends. I regretted being too busy, too stressed, too driven. I regretted never slowing down long enough to find out who *I* really was.

Sitting alone in my car that dark, drizzling night, I clutched a bottle of sleeping pills. Counting them out—two, four, six, eight... I was a nurse. I knew what it would take.

And then—three sharp knocks on my window. A woman appeared from nowhere. Her words jolted me back to reality: **"Are you okay?"** Tears streamed down my face as I shook my head. "No. I'm scared and lonely." She climbed into the car beside me. We talked. We cried. She got me through the night. It felt like divine intervention, speaking softly but firmly: "I'm not finished with you yet."

But the story didn't end there. Three months after that initial call, I received another one from Dr. Gazaleh. He cleared his throat and said, "Kathy... I'm not sure how to tell you this, but... all eight of your tests have come back negative.

» **You're not HIV positive." «**

As I hung up the phone, it felt like a thousand-pound weight was lifted from my chest. Some people call it a medical error; I call it a miracle. A double miracle. First, someone found me in my car right before I was about to end my life. And second, all my test results came back negative. I thought my life was over... and then, I got it back. I dropped to my knees, sobbing, and thanked God. In that moment, I made a vow: I will not live my life the same way ever again.

Staring death in the face shattered every illusion. The fear, the loneliness, the crushing regrets—it exposed how much of my life I'd spent sleepwalking, chasing things that didn't matter. That brush with death became my awakening. I saw, with painful clarity, that every moment is a gift—and I could no longer afford to waste a single one. From that day forward, I chose to live awake. To love deeper. Laugh louder. Stress less. And show up fully for the life I had nearly lost.

> **Tomorrow is never promised.
> But this moment? This moment is sacred.**

Now it's your turn to reflect...
What would you do if you were given a death sentence?

_____

_____

Would you have any regrets? What would they be?

_____

_____

Who would you want to talk to—or forgive—right now?

_____

_____

What have you been putting off that truly matters to you?

_____

_____

What is one thing you need to SHED to live more fully today?

_____

_____

Three R's of Shedding: Release. Reframe. Refocus.

When SHED HAPPENS, these three essential skills help you let go of what no longer serves you and move forward with clarity, confidence, and purpose.

1. Release the attachment.
"Attachment" sounds cozy and safe—like being connected to your mother by the umbilical cord. For nine months, that cord nurtured your growth. But eventually, the womb no longer served you. Nature knew it was time to shed. So, your mom was forced to "downsize" and release the attachment.

Attachments are only healthy for a season. Then, it's time to let go. Whether it's a toxic relationship, a job that's draining your soul, or a version of yourself you've outgrown—release it.

> **GOAL:** *Identify your emotional attachments—and release them quickly before they limit your growth.*

2. Reframe the situation.
Some changes may initially appear overwhelmingly negative, but with time most people recognize change is necessary or it's a blessing in disguise. Reframing — viewing a situation from a different perspective or a more positive light — is an essential skill.

Resilient people quickly see the positive side of change and don't allow a situation, no matter how bad, to get them stuck or derailed. Instead of it taking five years to get over a loss, maybe it only takes five months, five weeks, five days, five minutes or even five seconds.

Can you imagine what you were thinking when someone cut your cord? Talk about having a bad, bad, day! Now 30, 40, 50, 60+ years later you have been able to reframe the situation. You realize that the detachment gave you life. In reality, change, or the apparent loss, created space for something new to emerge.

Goal: *Develop a short reframe quotient by shedding negativity quickly and looking at change from the most positive light.*

---

3. Refocus your energy.
Your mind is powerful—but also noisy. When you're overwhelmed or distracted, hit pause. Return to your first survival skill: **breathe**. A deep, intentional breath resets your nervous system, re-centers your thoughts, and recharges your energy. Think about how much more energy could be harnessed if you were fully present and focused.

Here's a simple tool: use your **belly button** as a personal reset point. Touch it, breathe deeply, and bring yourself back to now. You'll dive deeper into this in the **SHED Button** chapter—a technique for quickly releasing, reframing, and refocusing. But this small action? It's a powerful beginning. One breath. One touch. One powerful return to now.

Goal: *Stay grounded in the present. Focus your energy where it counts—on the next right step.*

The Cycle of the 3 R's of Shedding

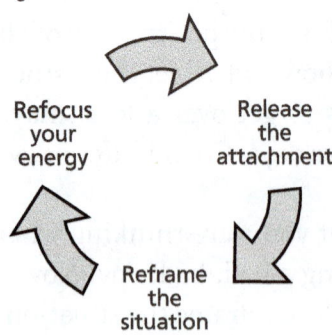

Part 1: Shedding

You can use the three R's of shedding for any challenging situation at work or in life. Practice them and they will become as easy and natural as riding a bike. Here is an example:

Challenging situation:
You get a flat tire on the way to work.

1. Release the attachment:
What do you need to detach from?
You are not going to be to work on time for your 8 a.m. meeting.

2. Reframe the situation:
How can I view this situation from the most positive light?
No one was in an accident. I am safe. I'm glad a have a cell phone.

3. Refocus your energy:
What action will I take to move forward?
Call work, tell them I will be late. Call AAA to come help me.

The Shedding Revolution's 5 Stages of Change
From Breakdown to Breakthrough

When SHED HAPPENS, change doesn't always knock politely, it often barges in uninvited. Whether subtle or seismic, most of us navigate a process of emotional evolution in its wake. Inspired by Elisabeth Kübler-Ross's powerful framework—*Denial, Anger, Bargaining, Depression, Acceptance*. The Shedding Revolution offers its own 5-stage path to healing, growth, and renewal.

Here are the 5 Stages of Change most people experience when letting go becomes necessary:

1	2	3	4	5
Loss	Anger	Discouragement	Acceptance	Celebration

1. Loss

Every shedding season starts here. A loss. Sometimes it's small, a flat tire, a missed opportunity, a canceled trip. But other times, the loss is life-altering: the death of a loved one, a divorce, an unexpected health diagnosis, or being forced into early retirement. For some, it's the quiet ache of becoming an empty nester or losing a sense of identity after caregiving for years.

Loss often brings fear—fear of the unknown, of what's next, of who you are without that role, that person, that plan.

But here's the truth: **you can't SHED what you won't acknowledge**. Recognize the loss. Feel it. Honor it. It's the gateway to everything that comes next.

2. Anger

Next comes the fire. And yes—it's okay to feel angry. You might be furious at your circumstances, at a broken system, or at life itself for pulling the rug out. You may even find yourself angry at God—or blaming yourself.

Maybe your retirement plans were shattered by a volatile stock market. That your health failed you despite your best efforts. Or maybe you were always the "strong one," and now feel forgotten in your own grief.

Other times, the anger turns inward. We blame ourselves, replaying what-ifs and should-haves until we're emotionally exhausted.

Anger is a natural response to loss, but what matters most is what you do with it. This is where forgiveness becomes essential. Not a feeling, but a bold decision to stop blaming yourself or others, release the grip of resentment, and begin to heal. Forgiveness turns pain into power and fire into fuel. It frees you from the past so you can finally move forward.

But not everyone makes that leap right away. Sometimes, when anger lingers unresolved, it doesn't explode—it implodes.

3. Discouragement
If anger is the flame, discouragement is the slow burn. **Unresolved anger can settle into a heaviness that feels like sadness, apathy, or even depression.** This is especially true when you've "done everything right"—raised the kids, paid the bills, contributed to your 401(k)—and still, life throws you a curveball.

Maybe your spouse passed away, and you're navigating grief and loneliness in a home that now feels too quiet. Maybe you were pushed out of your career earlier than expected and feel discarded after years of loyalty and hard work. You may be wondering: *Was it all for nothing?*

Discouragement whispers, *What's the point?* But this stage, while painful, is also powerful. It invites us to pause, reflect, and begin the slow, beautiful work of redefining what life can still be. Because even in the ashes, something new can grow.

4. Acceptance
Here comes the exhale. **This is the moment you stop resisting what is.** Not because you agree with it or wanted it to happen—but because you're ready to make peace with it.

Acceptance doesn't mean everything's fine. It means you've decided to stop pouring energy into what you can't change and start investing in what you can.

Maybe you've accepted your body's new pace. Or your solo status. Or that the career you thought you'd retire from ended early—but you still have more to give. Acceptance is where the fog begins to lift, and clarity returns.

5. Celebration
This stage may feel surprising, especially after significant loss. And for some, the word *celebration* might feel out of reach for a long time.

Some never get there... That's okay. As for me, the work towards joy is worth the try. There's no timeline, and no pressure to feel joy before your heart is ready.

But over time, something subtle can begin to shift. A softening. A glimmer of light in the dark. You begin to notice strength where there once was only sorrow. You begin to see how far you've come—how you kept showing up, even on the hardest days.

Celebration, in this context, isn't about "moving on." It's about honoring what was and recognizing what has quietly grown within you, perhaps deeper compassion, fresh perspective, or a clearer sense of what truly matters.

It doesn't mean you forget the pain. It means you've found the gift in it. You've grown. You've changed. And you're no longer who you were, you're someone wiser, braver, more beautifully alive.

And that, too, is worth honoring.

The EKG of Change
These stages are not a checklist. You won't move through them in a straight line. Think of the process more like an abnormal EKG—up and down. You may revisit stages. You may bounce between them. And that's okay.

Part 1: Shedding

The goal isn't to "hurry up and get through it." The goal is to keep moving, keep shedding, and keep growing—without getting stuck in any one stage. Because the Shedding Revolution™ isn't just about what you've lost. It's about who you're becoming.

The summary chart of the stages of change shows you how people think, feel, and behave at each stage. Suggestions are given for each change: What questions can be asked and what helps people move through the stages more successfully?

Shedding Revolution's 5 Stages of Change

Stage	Think	Feel	Behavior	Ask?	What helps?
Loss	No, not me!	Numb, fearful	Paralyzed, denial	What's the worst thing that could happen?	Acknowledge fears and emotions
Anger	Why me?	Anger, resentment	Resistance, bargaining	What information can I obtain?	Information, plan with options
Discouragement	Poor me…	Sad, overwhelmed	Unproductive, withdrawn	Can I hold on to the belief that the current challenge is creating space for something new to emerge?	Stay focused, prioritize, manage personal energy, explore possibilities
Acceptance	Ok me!	Content, re-energized	Productive, helpful	What is the best thing that could happen?	Ask, share and integrate lessons learned
Celebration	Yes me!	Excited	Throw a party	How can I share the gift with others	Helping others

Overcoming Fear: The Biggest Barrier to Shedding

Let's be honest. The two biggest fears most people carry with them are *dying*… and *public speaking*. And I've got news for you.

I've been a motivational speaker for 27 years—on stages across the country, speaking to audiences from hospitals to Fortune 500s. And I'm still scared to death of public speaking. Yep. Me. Still afraid.

You're Not Dead Yet!

You'd never guess that, would you? Most people don't. They see the confidence, the stage presence, the laughter, the energy. But they don't see the butterflies that set up camp in my stomach before every talk. So... how do I deal with it? **I don't show up.**

No, seriously. *I* don't walk out on stage. Someone else introduces me. They'll say something like: "Ladies and gentlemen, although she is a highly respected thought leader, author, and speaker, some people still question her strange ongoing relationship with a guy named... Lenny."

Suddenly, the lights go out. Floodlights sweep the room. Suspenseful music plays. And from the very back of the room, a figure emerges—wandering, confused, calling out: "Lenny? Lenny? Has anyone seen Lenny?" That's me.

I wander through the aisles asking if anyone's seen my sidekick, Lenny—he tends to vanish right before showtime and, for the record, holds a PhD in mischief. A giant image flashes on the screen. And there he is. Yep—Lenny's a lizard.

Don't worry, you're not hallucinating. This is how we roll. He's small, scaly, and somehow still manages to steal every show.

I then ask, "Could someone please turn the lights back on? We need everyone's help to find him!" The audience stands. The search begins. Lenny is, as usual, hiding under someone's chair. And just like that, the fear evaporates. Because I didn't try to hide from it. I danced with it. I gave it a name. I gave it a face. I made it fun.

You know who else did that? **Walt Disney**. Years ago, I had the privilege of speaking for The Disney Corporation in Orlando. I got to go behind the scenes—an incredible backstage tour. And I was stunned to learn that Walt Disney himself... was terrified of mice. So, what did he do? He embraced his fear, made it his *fun friend*. Big ears. Playful eyes. A cheerful smile. He named his fear Mickey. That mouse changed the world.

Part 1: Shedding

So, this isn't just about your comfort. It's about your contribution. Have you ever been to Disney?

My guess is about 98% of you just nodded or smiled. Maybe you remember spinning teacups, fireworks, laughter, sticky-fingered joy, or family vacations that still live in your photo albums. Now imagine if Walt Disney hadn't faced his fear of mice.

No Mickey.
No Disney World.
No memories.
No magic.
All of it... gone.

Because one person didn't embrace his fear. That's the hidden cost of fear—it doesn't just steal from you. It steals from everyone your life could have touched. So, ask yourself: **What magic might never exist because you didn't embrace your fear?**

Fear is normal. But letting it win? That's optional. Take the stage. Write the book. Take the trip. Speak the truth. Even if your knees shake or your voice trembles— embrace your fear. You might just change someone's world.

What is your biggest fear?

 **LENNY'S WISDOM:**
Fear is just excitement in a bad outfit. Give it a makeover and go.

SHED Management

Control Management

So, when SHED HAPPENS, we definitely need to develop a plan, which starts with goals and then continues with detailed instructions of how we are going to overcome the obstacles or deal with the challenges we are facing.

Assess your degree of control.
Control varies with each situation we experience. It's important to be aware of what we can control and what we can't control, because if we spend too much time focusing on situations that we can't control, we'll just grow weary and give up.

One of the biggest challenges people encounter when SHED HAPPENS is summarized well in the familiar Serenity Prayer:

Grant me the serenity to accept the things that I cannot change, courage to change the things I can, and wisdom to know the difference.

On one end of the scale we have full control. On the other end, we have no control. Somewhere in the middle we have some influence over a situation.

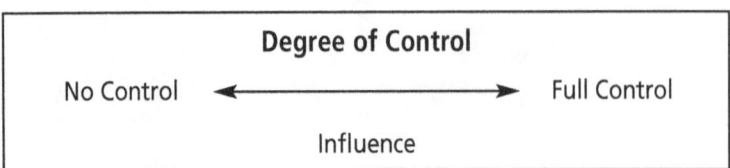

Part 1: Shedding

The goal is to clearly understand where the degree of control is in each situation. Evaluate whether you have:
1. No Control
2. Influence
3. Control

Where do most of us waste our energy? On situations that we have no control over.

Let's use the example of your negative friend. Look at the following chart. As you can see there are parts where you have control, influence, and no control.

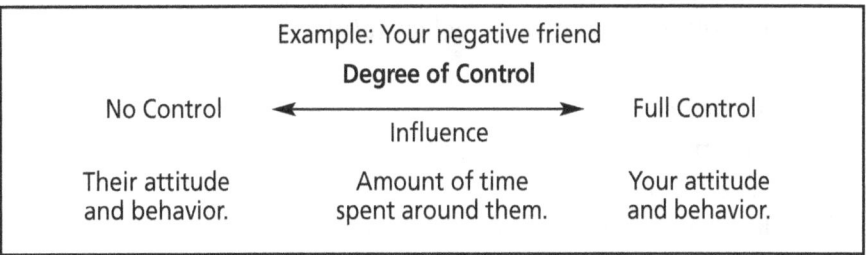

Therefore, we need to train ourselves to focus only on what we can control or what we have some influence over, and develop a well-thought-out, written plan accordingly. Once you've developed this plan to tackle the challenges you are facing, you then need to execute the plan and take the necessary action steps that you believe will help you overcome them.

Fill out the control chart below. Depending on your SHED HAPPENS, you may identify different areas of no control, influence, or control.

Identify your SHED HAPPENS_____

No Control	Influence	Control

LENNY'S WISDOM:
If you can't control it, don't carry it. I don't drag around other lizards' tails.

25 Things You Can Control Right Now
Mindset & Mood
1. What you focus on: problems or possibilities
2. How much you worry about things you can't control
3. The ratio of positive to negative thoughts you allow
4. How you talk to yourself (inner critic or inner coach?)
5. How much time you spend in the present moment—the NOW
6. What you believe about yourself and your future
7. How often you pause to feel grateful, even in chaos

Body & Energy
8. How much sleep you get (bedtime is your superpower)
9. The kind of food you eat, fuel or filler?
10. How often you move your body: walk, stretch, dance, shake
11. What you drink—hydration or habit?
12. How you treat your body: with kindness or criticism
13. When you rest and recharge without guilt
14. How much screen time you allow yourself (scroll or soul?)

People & Presence
15. Who you choose to spend your time with
16. How often you say, "thank you" and mean it
17. How well you listen, with your ears and your heart
18. How you deal with anger—explode, suppress, or express wisely
19. Who you forgive, and how quickly you stop carrying their baggage
20. How open you are to connection, even when it feels vulnerable
21. Whether you set healthy boundaries or burn out trying to please

Action & Attitude
22. Whether you keep complaining or start changing

Part 1: Shedding

23. How quickly you practice the 3 R's of Shedding: Release, Reframe, Refocus
24. What you cling to—and what you're willing to shed
25. How fully you show up in the NOW

Energy Management: Stop the Leak, Fuel the Life

If life is a marathon, then energy—not time—is your most precious resource. You can't pour from an empty cup, yet most of us leak energy every day without realizing it. Some experts believe energy—not politics, not economics—is the most urgent survival issue of our time. And while we might not solve the global energy crisis, we can absolutely start managing our personal power grid.

Stop the Leak

If Eckhart Tolle is even close to right when he says 93% of our thoughts are repetitive and useless, we're hemorrhaging energy—mentally, emotionally, and physically.

Top culprits?
- Toxic people
- Negative self-talk
- Worry loops
- Regret
- Resentment

Every time we engage in these, we're plugging into a drain, not a charger. So, the first rule of energy management is simple: Stop the leak. Choose your inputs and your inner dialogue with care.

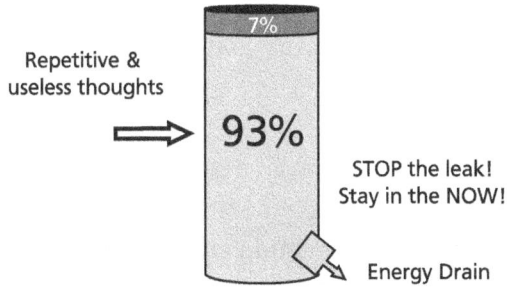

Take a Personal Energy Audit
Before you go further, take a few moments to reflect on what fuels you—and what drains you. This simple exercise can reveal more than you might expect.

Use the chart below to list your energy boosters and energy drainers—people, activities, thoughts, habits, or environments. Be honest and specific.

Gives Me Energy	Drains My Energy
(e.g., time in nature, music, friends who lift me up)	(e.g., negative self-talk, clutter, certain people)

Once complete, ask yourself:
What can I do more of?
What can I let go of, or limit, to protect my energy?

Stay Above the Acceptance Line
All emotions carry energy. Some fuel us. Others deplete us.
- Joy, gratitude, and love? High-octane fuel.
- Anger, fear, and shame? Major drains.
- Acceptance? The neutral zone—it won't charge you, but it won't drain you either.

You don't have to shout "Wahoo!" every time life hands you lemons. But if you can aim to keep your emotional state at acceptance or higher, you'll conserve energy and think more clearly.

Part 1: Shedding

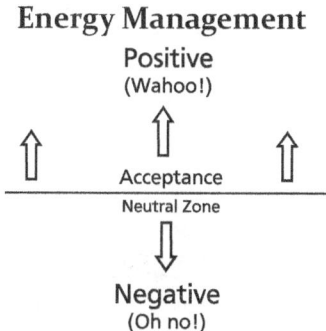

Of course, no one can stay in high-vibe energy all the time. Even with awareness, life throws its "Oh no!" moments. And that's where this next SHED skill comes in...

Above-the-Neck Constipation: Clear It Before You Clog Up
Want a surprising source of energy drain? It's not just the people around you—it's the mental mess stuck between your ears.

I call it Above-the-Neck Constipation. You know what I'm talking about: that stinking thinking, the negativity, worry loops, emotional junk food. The pressure builds, and the #1 symptom shows up fast: **complaining**.

Here's a stat that might blow your circuits: The average person complains **15–30 times a day**. On Mondays? We spend **34 minutes just venting**. That's a full episode of negativity reruns—with zero uplift.

Complaining drains your brain, leaks your energy, and infects the people around you. That's why I wear a bracelet that says: **"I'm Allergic to Negativity."** (And I'm not alone—thousands of people wear them now. And one division of the Mayo Clinic actually made it part of their *uniform!*)

When someone on staff starts being negative, they snap their wristband and say:
SHED UP!
SHED the negativity, and keep your positive attitude UP!

Playful. Powerful. And it works. Jacqueline Jenkins, Director of Nursing, Mayo Clinic said after implementing *SHED for Success*™: "Our employee engagement jumped from 40% to 60% in six months."

So, what's the cure? **A mental enema**.

And the five **SHED Skills** are your go-to flush. These skills aren't just nice ideas—they're tools to unclog your mind and free your focus:
1. **SHED the Complaint Habit** – Swap griping for gratitude or curiosity.
2. **Avoid Toxic People** – Negativity is contagious. Limit exposure like secondhand smoke.
3. **Stop the Negative Tapes** – If your mind's stuck in a bad loop (I'm not good enough, smart enough, young enough) press pause and reframe.
4. **Focus on What's Right** – Energy flows where your attention goes.
5. **Remember: The Gas Will Pass** – Some stress just needs to be released, not recycled.

> **LENNY'S WISDOM:**
> *You can't graduate life with honors if you're majoring in drama. Drop the class. SHED the negativity.*

Take a Two-Minute Time Out

Let's face it, as we know now—SHED HAPPENS. You spill your coffee. Miss an important call. Get blindsided by bad news. These "Oh no!" moments are part of life, and they come without warning. When they do, give yourself permission to pause, not power through. This isn't a punishment. It's a power move. A two-minute ritual to feel your feelings, move the energy, and choose your next step with intention.

Here's how it works:
1. **Say it out loud:**
   "Oh no. SHED HAPPENED." (Yes, say it. Even in your head. Naming it gives it shape—so you can move it.)

2. **Feel it—then *move* it.**
   Let the emotion come. Frustration. Sadness. Confusion. Don't numb it—**channel** it. Hit a pillow. Do 20 jumping jacks. Go for a walk. Scream into a towel. Punch a couch cushion (not your spouse). Energy gets trapped in your body. Physical motion helps release it.
3. **Name the loss.**
   What were you hoping for that didn't happen? What got SHED that you weren't ready to let go of?
4. **Take one small action.**
   Ask: *What's the next best thing I can do right now?* Not the perfect thing. Not the final fix. Just the next right step.
5. **Rise back to acceptance—or higher.**
   The goal isn't to feel fantastic. It's to feel **free**. Even a half-step up the energy ladder is progress. That's you building your SHED muscle.

> **LENNY'S WISDOM:**
> *When SHED HAPPENS, don't bottle it up—shake it off, shout it out, stomp it through. Energy that moves becomes energy you can use.*

Build Your SHED Muscle

Think of this like doing emotional push-ups. The more often you practice these tiny resets, the more emotional strength and flexibility you'll build. So, the next time life throws a curveball, you'll be ready. Not perfect. Not invincible. Just centered, capable, and more in control than you think. Two minutes. One choice. Infinite impact.

Recharge Every 90 Minutes

Your body operates on what's called an Ultradian rhythm, cycles of high focus followed by natural dips every 90–120 minutes. According to researcher, Ernest Rossi, during those dips, your body needs a 20-minute reset to repair and refuel.

Ignoring this rhythm doesn't make you strong, it makes you susceptible to burnout, brain fog, and emotional reactivity.

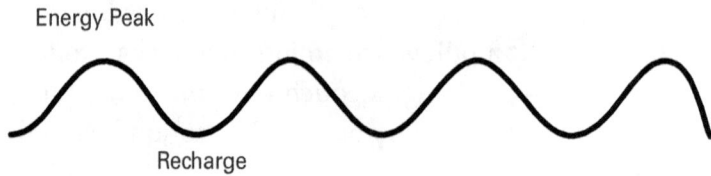

Our Body's Ultradian Cycle

Every 90 minutes

Warning signs it's time to recharge:
- Yawning or sighing
- Restlessness or need to stretch
- Craving snacks
- Difficulty concentrating
- Trouble finding the right word
- Frequent bathroom urges

These aren't weaknesses, they're built-in biological cues. When we override them, we pay the price. Whether it's a snap at a loved one, brain fog during a conversation, or complete emotional collapse later, the energy debt adds up.

Think Like a Battery, Not a Machine
You wouldn't try to shock a heart with a defibrillator that wasn't charged. (Believe it or not, I've seen it happen.) Your body is no different. Push too long without a recharge, and you'll hit emotional or physical flatline. So, the better question is: Why not work *with* your natural rhythm instead of against it?

Recharge Reminders
- Don't ignore the signals. Your body knows. Listen.
- Take real breaks every 90–120 minutes. Step away. Breathe. Move.
- Set boundaries. "No" is a full sentence and a sacred one.
- Honor your energy peaks and valleys. Ride the waves, don't fight them.
- You're not lazy for resting. You're human—and smart for managing your energy like it matters.

Part 1: Shedding

 **LENNY'S WISDOM:**
You're not Wi-Fi. Stop trying to stay connected to everything. SHED and recharge.

44 Instant Energy Boosters

Five minutes or less. Almost anywhere. Pick one and power up.

Breathe + Recenter
1. Take 2–3 deep cleansing breaths (your first life skill!)
2. Splash water on your face
3. Smile, even a fake one counts
4. Rub your hands together
5. Massage your eyes and temples
6. Use self-acupressure (squeeze your thumb or between your brows)
7. Sniff citrus, lavender, or peppermint
8. Hug yourself
9. Take a two-minute time out (see previous section!)
10. Look in the mirror and say something kind. "You're awesome!" works.

Move It, Boost It
11. Do 10 jumping jacks
12. Stand up and stretch, reach high, bend low
13. Stomp your feet 10 times (wake up those nerves)
14. Roll up and down on your toes
15. Take a short walk, even around the room
16. Switch your chair or change sitting position
17. Change your shoes—or take them off
18. Dance it out (even silently!)

Mood Magic
19. Laugh—watch a 30-second funny clip or replay a hilarious memory

20. Tell a joke (even a bad one)
21. Text someone you miss
22. Give a compliment
23. Write a kind note
24. Engage with a positive person
25. Do a random act of kindness
26. Make a gratitude list
27. List 3 things you've accomplished today—no matter how small
28. Say thank you to someone (even silently)

Snack Smart
29. Drink a tall glass of water
30. Eat a healthy power snack (apple slices, trail mix, etc.)
31. Enjoy a handful of nuts
32. Munch on some berries
33. Have a mint
34. Eat some yogurt
35. Savor a cup of tea (especially green or herbal)
36. Treat yourself to a piece of dark chocolate (a piece, not a pound!)

Engage Your Senses
37. Sing your favorite song (belt it or hum it)
38. Listen to a tune you love
39. Smell a calming essential oil
40. Put on a bright accessory (scarf, earrings, socks—whatever pops!)
41. Gaze at an inspiring or calming photo
42. Touch something soft or grounding (a smooth rock, cozy fabric)
43. Light a candle or adjust the lighting
44. Doodle, scribble, or color just for fun

Pro Tip: *Pick your favorite five and post them somewhere you'll see every day. Your energy is precious. Protect it. Boost it. Own it.*

Negative Rechargers: The Cost of Quick Fixes

When SHED HAPPENS—when life knocks the wind out of you—it's natural to reach for something that brings relief. Something to numb the pain, quiet the noise, or make you feel powerful again. Sometimes, these "go-to" behaviors seem to *recharge* us... but only at first. I call them **Negative Rechargers**.

They do give you a burst of energy, release, or control—but that surge comes at a steep price. These are the things that feel like comfort or escape in the moment but often leave you (and those around you) feeling worse in the long run. They may work temporarily. But they don't restore you. They **drain your soul's battery** faster than they fill it.

Common Negative Rechargers:
- **Taking drugs or excessive drinking** – numbs the pain but creates deeper wounds
- **Overeating or bingeing on sugar/salt/fat** – comfort that turns into self-sabotage
- **Smoking** – a breath of relief with a long-term cost to your body
- **Hurting others physically or verbally** – momentary control that fractures relationships
- **Yelling, bullying, or being mean** – false power fueled by fear or grief
- **Withdrawing and isolating** – safety that quickly becomes a prison
- **Overplaying video games or watching too much TV** – distraction that detaches you from real life
- **Oversleeping** – escape from life's messes that makes them pile up
- **Self-harm** – a desperate cry for control that deepens the pain
- **Breaking things or destroying property** – outward chaos that reflects inner turmoil
- **Criticizing others or cheating on someone** – attempts to feel superior or seen, rooted in inner emptiness

These behaviors don't make you "bad." They make you *human*—but hurting. They signal that something needs attention. Something needs to be SHED, reframed, and healed. So next time you find yourself reaching for a negative recharger, pause. Ask yourself: "Is this really recharging me... or just temporarily relieving me?"

You deserve real recharge. Not a spark that burns you. A light that lifts you.

 **LENNY'S WISDOM:**
If your "recharge" leaves you feeling worse, that's not self-care—it's self-sabotage in a fuzzy bathrobe.

Learning to Say NO: How One Word Can Save Your Life

It sounds simple, but for many of us, it's one of the hardest things to do. As toddlers, we had no problem saying it. "NO!" was our favorite word. But somewhere along the way, we learned to trade our truth for approval. We became conditioned to say yes—even when every fiber of our being screamed otherwise. Saying "no" got labeled as selfish. But here's what I learned the hard way: Saying no is not a rejection. It's a boundary. A declaration. A lifeline.

The Day I Almost Died Because I Couldn't Say NO

In 1988, I was running on fumes. I'd worked back-to-back double shifts in the ER. I was bone-tired, emotionally spent, and dangerously disconnected from my own body. As I clocked in for another 7 a.m. shift, my manager Linda rushed over.

"Kathy, someone called out. We need you to stay another double. Please. The ER is overwhelmed. There's no one else." My soul was screaming *NO*. But my mouth said *YES*.

That day was relentless—car wrecks, gunshot wounds, cardiac arrests. I barely had time to breathe. After 16+ hours, I finally left the ER, exhausted, disoriented, and running on empty. It was dark. It was raining. And I was beyond functioning.

Part 1: Shedding

I ran a stop sign and slammed into the side of a speeding 18-wheeler. I shouldn't have survived. But I did.

And as I lay in the back of an ambulance, being rushed back to the ER I had just left, I realized the true cause of the accident: **My inability to say NO.**

Yes, I had a concussion. Cuts. Bruises. But the most dangerous injury? Was invisible. It was my chronic, unexamined compulsion to say YES. To over-give. To over-perform. To over-function.

It forced me to SHED the belief that I had to save everyone—even at the cost of myself. Now, **I know that saying NO is a sacred act**. One that protects your peace, your purpose, and your life.

5 Questions to Ask Before You Say YES
1. **What are your boundaries—physically, emotionally, mentally?**
   Know your limits. Violating them comes at a cost.
2. **Will saying YES increase your stress or reduce it?**
   If it spikes your stress, that's a red flag. If it nourishes you, it might be worth your yes.
3. **Are you saying YES out of guilt, fear, or a need for approval?**
   If so, pause. Those are rarely healthy motivations.
4. **Does it really require an urgent response?**
   No? Then give yourself time. Sleep on it. Reflect.
5. **Are you clear on your priorities?**
   When you know what deserves your YES, your No becomes much easier.

7 Ways to Say NO Without Guilt
1. "Thank you for thinking of me, but I need to say NO right now to honor my energy."
2. "I'm already committed elsewhere, and I want to give my best to that."

3. "That doesn't align with my priorities at the moment."
4. "I'm at capacity—I wouldn't be able to do it well."
5. "Let me think about it and get back to you." *(Buy yourself time.)*
6. "I'm practicing saying no more often—this is one of those times."
7. "NO, but here's another person or option you might try."

LENNY'S WISDOM:
"No" is a full sentence. Add a smile if you're over 50 and done people-pleasing.

Be in the NOW Management: Manage the NOW, Change Your Life

If you want to change your life, there's only one place to start: Right here. Right now. Not yesterday. Not someday. Not after the kids grow up, or you lose ten pounds, or Mercury is out of retrograde. Just... NOW.

Even when *SHED HAPPENS*, the present moment is where your real power lives. It's messy. It's beautiful. It can be wildly uncomfortable. But it's real—and it's the **only moment** you've actually got.

We spend so much time looping through regrets from the past or stressing over some imaginary disaster in the future. Then add in all the notifications, emails, and distractions—and it's no wonder we miss the moment we're actually living in.

Eckhart Tolle said it best: "93% of our thoughts are repetitive and useless." Let that sink in. Nearly all of your thinking... is noise. So, what do we do? We stay in the NOW. Even when it's uncomfortable. Even when it sucks. Because the only way through it... is *through it*.

Remember that chapter about fear? About how Lenny reminded me that fear doesn't have to be so scary? Well, here's where that lesson comes home.

Part 1: Shedding

Fear lives in the future.
Freedom lives in the now.

You can't outrun fear by fast-forwarding through life. You face it—right here, right now.

That's what shedding is really about. It's not about pretending everything's fine—it's about growing through the tough stuff. And yes, it's a process. Real growth usually happens in **baby steps**, not dramatic leaps.

Your Breath: First Aid for Fear and Anxiety
Pause. Breathe in slowly. Breathe out even slower.

This simple act activates your parasympathetic nervous system, calming your body and clearing your mind. You don't need 21 days to change a habit or a perfect morning routine. You just need this moment. And a breath.

Breath Break: Tap Into Your SHED Button
Challenge: Place your right hand gently over your belly button. (Lenny likes to call this your *SHED button*—after all, it was your first shedding moment when your umbilical cord was cut!)

Now, take a deep breath in through your nose. Let your belly rise like a balloon filling with air.

Hold for 4 seconds...

Then, exhale slowly through your mouth, allowing your body to soften and release.

» **Repeat this three times.** «

Why it matters:
- It brings you back to NOW.
- It increases oxygen to your brain, improving memory, clarity, and calmness.
- It resets your nervous system and reconnects you to yourself.
- It's your body's built-in reset button, always with you, always ready.

You've known how to do this since the day you were born. Your first act of life was a breath. So next time SHED HAPPENS... Come back to the NOW. Come back to your breath. Because when you manage the NOW—you manage your life.

LENNY'S WISDOM:
When SHED HAPPENS, before you reach for anything else, try a breath—it's your built-in pharmacy.

The Big Three: Shedding Roles, Stuff and Stories

Letting go isn't easy, especially when what you're shedding is tied to your identity, your memories, or your sense of home.

There are three primary attachments that humans struggle to SHED:
- The **roles** we play
- The **stuff** we accumulate
- The **stories** that shape the **beliefs** we cling to

These aren't just things we carry—they often carry us. But what happens when we outgrow them, or life asks us to release them before we're ready? Let's take a closer look at each:

1. Roles
We get attached to our roles—and often over-identify with them. "I am a nurse." "I'm a mom." "I'm a spouse." "I'm a business owner." But those roles are just temporary costumes we wear in the play of life. Necessary? Often. Meaningful? Definitely. But permanent? **Almost Never.** Even your role as a mom might end or morph as your children

Part 1: Shedding

grow older. When we lose a role—whether through job loss, divorce, or death—it can feel like we've lost ourselves. And that's because our roles often come bundled with beliefs, routines, relationships, and... stuff. Roles change. But your *worth* doesn't.

2. Stuff

Humans get attached to stuff. My house. My car. My grandmother's vase. Anytime you hear the word *"my"*, it's a signal—attachment detected. When I decided to sell my house, I called a real estate agent and asked, "What's the biggest challenge in helping people sell?" She didn't even blink. "Oh, that's easy. **People don't know what to do with their STUFF!.**"

She was right. I took a look around and realized how much I was holding on to. Sentimental knickknacks. Clothes I hadn't worn in years. Boxes in the attic I hadn't opened since the Clinton administration. So, I grabbed a timer. Just 15 minutes. I picked an area of my closet—that felt manageable. When the timer went off, I felt a little lighter and energized—so I set it again. And again. Four rounds later, I'd filled three big bags of clothes and dropped them off at Goodwill. It was a surprisingly emotional process—but deeply freeing.

NOTE: And for those of us navigating life after 50, the shedding doesn't stop—it accelerates. First, we downsize from the big family home to a smaller house or condo. Then maybe to a retirement center. Eventually, maybe we're faced with one small room. It's not just about deciding what to keep—because the deeper truth is this: **everything we own and everyone we love; we will SHED one day**. That's the reality. And each phase of life invites us to practice the art of letting go—with grace, courage, and love. It's a slow, sacred stripping down. And yes—it's painful. But it can also be powerful. Because in the process of letting go, you begin to uncover what *truly* matters.

Ready to SHED Your Stuff?

We all have too much. Too much weight. Too many decisions. Too many dusty "someday" items cluttering our space *and* our spirit.

You're Not Dead Yet!

"Darling daughter, all this will be yours one day."

Here's a simple tool to get started:

SHED Your Stuff Checklist

Let go of what weighs you down. One shelf, one section, one story at a time.

Get Started
- Set a 15-minute timer.
- Choose ONE small area:
  - Closet section
  - Drawer
  - Shelf
  - Cabinet
  - Nightstand
  - Pantry or fridge
  - Purse or backpack
  - Garage corner or car trunk

Ask the SHED Questions:
- Have I worn or used this in the past year?
- Does this bring me joy?
- Would someone else benefit more from this?

Let It Go:
- Donate
- Trash/Recycle
- Gift to someone who needs it
- Sell it

Celebrate:
- Check in: How do I feel?
- Reward yourself: a massage, bubble bath, text a friend
- Want more momentum? Set the timer again!

Pro Tip: *"You're not just shedding stuff—you're shedding stress, decision fatigue, and emotional clutter."*

---

3. Stories/Beliefs

Our beliefs are the stories we tell ourselves about how the world works—or *should* work. "That's just the way we've always done it." "Kids today just don't get it." "I liked it better when you could just pick up the phone and talk to a human instead chat with a robot." Beliefs are comforting because they give us a sense of certainty. But when the world changes—and it always does—clinging to outdated beliefs can become a source of frustration, bitterness, or disconnection. Letting go of an old belief doesn't mean betraying your values. It means updating your operating system so you can function in the present.

When Losses Compound

Sometimes, we don't just lose one thing, we lose many at once. Say you lose a job. That's the role. But you may also lose the stuff that came with it (income, house, status). And the belief system you had around security? That might go, too. That's why shedding is such a vital life skill. When one thread unravels, you need tools to keep from falling apart.

Shedding Expectations

In 2005, I volunteered to spend a month in Africa taking care of orphans who had lost their parents to AIDS. I was overwhelmed to discover there were over 12,000 orphans just in the small city of Ndola, Zambia. During an afternoon visit with the local bishop, I inquired about how the orphans could be so happy, so full of joy while they had nothing?

"They have no expectations," he replied.

"They have no expectation of getting an education, no expectation of having parents and no expectation of having a home."

We all have our reference points. To the African AIDS orphans, our shrinking 401K statements would be like winning the lottery!

A survey cited in Psychology Today revealed Americans are becoming more depressed than ever before. Researchers believe the phenomenon is closely linked to the unrealistic expectations of the American Dream. The more people focus on a materialistic pathway to happiness, the less happy they tend to be.

Now, there is nothing wrong with having expectations. Expectations can propel us to dream, set goals and accomplish things in life. Unnecessary pain and suffering arises when we over attach to our expectations. Learning to realistically revisit and adjust them appropriately will enhance your ability to SHED.

CAUTION: Expectations can be spoken or unspoken. Our expectations, shaped by our current reality and past experiences, greatly influence our ability to adapt to change.

LENNY'S WISDOM:
Expectations can be like tight pants—uncomfortable, unrealistic, and often split under pressure.

Helping Kids SHED

Kids are natural shedders. Just watch a toddler move from bottle to sippy cup, from crawling to walking, from babbling to full sentences. They grow quickly, physically, emotionally, and mentally, and every stage requires letting go of the old to embrace the new.

But over time, that natural rhythm can get disrupted. Change starts to feel scary. Loss becomes confusing. And unless we guide them through it, kids begin clinging to habits, identities, or relationships that no longer serve them. That's where the SHED philosophy comes in.

To help kids SHED well:
- **Start with feelings.**
  Teach kids to recognize the four core emotions—**happy, sad, angry, and scared**. These are the building blocks of emotional intelligence. When kids can name what they feel, they're more equipped to move through it.

- **Normalize mixed emotions.**
  Let kids know it's completely normal to have several feelings at once. One may feel strongest, but others often show up too.

  Example: A child whose parents are getting divorced may feel:
  1. **Sad** – "My parents aren't married anymore."
  2. **Happy** – "At least they don't fight all the time now."
  3. **Angry** – "Why are my friends' parents still together?"
  4. **Scared** – "What will happen to me? Will my parents stop loving me?"

- **Create a safe space for expression.**
  Ask open-ended questions. Let them share without fixing or judging. Help them explore both what they're letting go of—and what they're growing into.

- **Model healthy shedding.**
  Kids and grandkids are always watching. Let them see you navigating change with honesty, grace, and a little humor. Show them that it's okay to feel uncertain—and that shedding is a normal, lifelong process.

- **Mark transitions with meaning.**
  Celebrate milestones. Hold simple rituals for goodbyes. Write farewell letters to pets, friends, or even toys. These acts help kids release emotions and honor the moment.

- **Remind them: Shedding is growth.**
  Let them know that shedding doesn't mean losing who they are, it means becoming who they're meant to be.

The earlier kids learn that change isn't something to fear, the more resilient, grounded, and courageous they'll become. Let's teach them how to SHED—strong, healthy, and from the heart.

As kids learn to SHED—whether it's fears, friendships, or old versions of themselves—they need simple, practical tools to help them handle the emotions that come with change.

Emotional CPR is a powerful practice for tending to your inner world. Think of it as first aid for the heart—a way to recognize, manage, and release emotions in healthy ways, especially when *SHED HAPPENS*. It helps you stay grounded during life's inevitable storms and builds the muscle of emotional resilience.

But let's be clear: Emotional CPR is for adults first. We can't teach what we haven't practiced. When grown-ups learn to recognize, manage, and release their own emotions in healthy ways, they model emotional strength and resilience. And that's the real gift we pass on to the next generation.

Here's How Emotional CPR Works:
C is for Check in with Your Feelings
Just like checking the weather before heading outside, you need to check in with how you feel. As mentioned above, the four main feelings are **happy, sad, angry, and scared**. All feelings are valid, there's no right or wrong emotion. The goal is to notice what you're feeling, name it, and not get stuck in it. Feel it… and then let it flow.

P is for Plug in and Recharge
Your body and brain are like a phone, they need to be recharged to work properly. When you're dealing with tough emotions or changes, your energy gets drained faster. Find what helps you recharge: walking, drawing, talking, music, breathing, or just being quiet. Recharging helps you bounce back.

R is for Rely on Your 911 Support Team
No one gets through life alone, not even the strongest lizard (just ask Lenny). That's why it's essential to build your own **911 Support Team**: a group of people you can count on when SHED HAPPENS. Your team might include parents, children, friends, neighbors, counselors, even your pet.

NOTE: Each person on your team has a strength.
Some are listeners. Some are fixers. Some bring calm. Others bring snacks. What matters is knowing **who** to call—and **when**. Think of it like this: You wouldn't call your therapist for a leaking sink—you'd call a plumber. And if you had a 104-degree fever, you wouldn't dial up your funny friend, you'd need a doctor (or at least someone to drive you to urgent care).

The same principle applies to emotional emergencies, big decisions, and personal meltdowns. Knowing **who can help with what** can save you time, stress, and heartache.

Create Your 911 Support Team - Personal Advisory Board
Make a list of who you'd reach out to in different situations:
- For advice or perspective
- For emotional support
- For practical help
- For comfort or a good laugh
- For urgent, crisis-level support

Take a snapshot of the list and keep it in your phone, journal, or wallet—somewhere you can reach for it when things get overwhelming.

 **LENNY'S WISDOM:**
Asking for help isn't weak—it's wise. And brave. And very SHED-savvy.

Utilize Emotional CPR

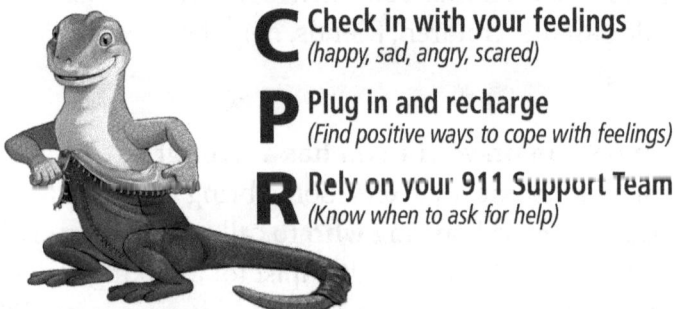

C Check in with your feelings
(happy, sad, angry, scared)

P Plug in and recharge
(Find positive ways to cope with feelings)

R Rely on your 911 Support Team
(Know when to ask for help)

Part 1: Shedding

911 Support Team/Personal Advisory Board

AREAS OF YOUR LIFE	PERSONS	STRENGTH	CONTACT INFORMATION
FAMILY			
FRIENDS			
Humor friend			
Non-human friend (pets)			
PROFESSIONALS			
Doctor			
Dentist			
Spritual Advisor			
Counselor			
Financial advisor			
Business/Career			
Lawyer			

You're Not Dead Yet!

PART 2
MORE LIFE SKILLS FOR LIVING WELL

KIM HARMS

Grappling With Grief

Grief is the price we pay for love.
— Queen Elizabeth II

Death, divorce, job loss, hurricanes, flooding, political unrest, health issues and economic difficulties are part of life. Those affected by loss are left in shock and grief frequently wondering how they can cope in the world that has been turned upside down. If you live in a third world country or a country experiencing war or unrest, you learn about loss and grief early. But if you live in a country at peace with a high life expectancy you get very little training in managing grief, particularly catastrophic grief.

Kathy covered valuable techniques for managing grief in the SHED section, but we both think that this topic deserves additional attention. Expecting a good life, as we typically do in the U.S., can make the management of loss even more difficult.

I have spent many years in the grief pit, and one thing I can tell you is that it is a dreadful place to live. After our son Eric died Jim and I found that we managed grief differently. Jim would constantly play old videos of Eric and he would sit in his room almost every night. I couldn't step into Eric's room for three years, and hearing his voice would send me into a panic. We had to work hard to honor each other's differences and fight with all of our might to work through the pain. Although it was a long process it was definitely worth it.

Some individuals may have more experience or personal strengths when it comes to coping with grief, which can help them recover more easily. Grief is a deeply personal journey—no two people experience or process it in exactly the same way, even if they've faced similar situations. We need to avoid judging others or placing expectations on how long someone "should" grieve. Some may move through the process more quickly or with less visible struggle. Ultimately, the only grief we can truly understand and manage is our own.

For a long time, grief wrapped itself around me like a net I couldn't escape—tight, suffocating, inescapable. Climbing out of that pit wasn't quick or easy. It took time. It took tears. It took determination I didn't know I had. But little by little, the grip loosened. And then, one day, I noticed it was no longer there. Grief still visits now and then—especially on anniversaries or unexpected moments—but it doesn't own me anymore. These days, when I smile, it's not just for show. It's real. My heart still remembers, it still aches sometimes, but has learned how to beat with joy again.

Tasks of Mourning

Grief and mourning are different things. Grief is the personal experience of the loss and mourning is the process that occurs after the loss. There are even tasks of mourning. Being the typical type A dentist, breaking mourning down into tasks with a definitive goal at the end is extremely helpful!

In 1982, William Worden published "Four Tasks of Mourning" suggesting that here are 4 tasks that must be completed before fully adapting to a loss.

The first task of mourning is to accept the reality of the loss. This may seem a simple thing, but when something unexpected and catastrophic occurs, it is sometimes difficult for the mind to adjust to reality.

The second task is to process the pain of grief. Keeping busy, crying, talking, seeking therapy, finding a support group or a cause are all ways to process the pain. This task is highly individualized, and it is important to make sure to work through the pain and not avoid it. Avoiding the pain can cause a person to get stuck in this task.

The third task of mourning is to adjust to the world that exists after the loss. New financial or social circumstances associated with the loss may be hard to face. It is sometimes helpful to develop new interests or even move to new surroundings. Before Eric died, I was passionate about photography (especially involving my children). After Eric died, I was unable to take pictures for a long time. Instead, I started to paint on porcelain, which was very therapeutic. The arrival of grandchildren (one of them named Eric) was immensely helpful. After Jim died, I had to adjust to being alone after 44 years. Becoming a widow demands the strength to rebuild your identity and the courage to seek out purpose and joy in a life forever changed.

The fourth and final task of mourning is to develop a lasting connection to your loss in a way that does not interfere with the process of embarking on your new life. This task involves living your present life without letting your past life interfere. It is a difficult task for most but extremely important. Many experience survivors' guilt, particularly after losing a loved one, and feel that being happy somehow betrays the love they felt. It is a false guilt. For me, establishing 65 Rwandan libraries in Eric's name helped with this task. Eric loved to read.

Genders differ.
Men and women frequently handle loss differently, which can cause a serious strain on relationships. The important thing to remember is to not judge each other and respect the differences. Trying to figure out "why" something happened can frequently lead you down a wormhole. Why did Eric die? Why do hurricanes happen? Why did your wife get cancer? Why did your spouse leave you? There are frequently no answers, and healing requires acceptance even without understanding the "why".

Men may find it more difficult to admit they are depressed. After Eric's death I accepted that I was suffering from depression and was treated. Yet, my husband Jim would not accept that he was depressed and was therefore not treated. However, a year after Eric died and two years after his heart checked out as healthy Jim required major heart surgery. He eventually died from his broken heart. Stress from grief and depression can have devastating effects on our cardiovascular system.

There is sometimes a stigma to being diagnosed and treated for depression. Why? The only side effect that I have from being treated for depression is that I am happier. My husband's valve replacement and quadruple bypass, followed by another valve replacement 6 years later, followed by his death was much more traumatic. Let's rethink this!

People with grief frequently have Post Traumatic Stress.

Frequently for a while, sometimes for an entire life, survivors of loss are bombarded by waves of grief at unexpected moments. Occasionally waves become tsunamis. For me, those waves came without warning and were frequently triggered by certain words, jazz music or a time of year. The two most frequent triggers for me were any mention of New York or Columbia. It is amazing how many times we hear the word New York in a day. Columbia is even worse! Columbia the University, Columbia Sportswear, Columbia SC, Columbia Missouri, Columbia Maryland, Columbia the country, Columbia River, Columbia Ice field, the space shuttle Columbia there is even an asteroid named Columbia. You can't get through the day without hearing about New York or Columbia; numerous times! Fortunately, for me, most of those triggers have dissipated.

Social anxiety is common after a catastrophic loss.

Going out in public after a loss can be difficult. The post-loss world looks very different from the pre-loss world. Watching people enjoying life was hard. I remember the horrible feeling I would have when I saw a family with three children because I no longer had three children. It was a very strange and embarrassing feeling. It also took about 5 years before I could go through an entire wedding without crying from despair instead of joy. Funerals were also hard.

Forgiveness is important.
One of the most powerful steps you can take toward emotional healing is choosing to forgive—others and yourself. Forgiveness doesn't excuse what happened; it simply sets your heart free. After Eric died, I traveled to Rwanda to help establish libraries in his memory and to learn more about grief recovery. What I didn't expect was to encounter a nation of forgiveness experts. In 1994, Rwanda endured one of the deadliest genocides in history—nearly a million people were killed by their own neighbors in just 100 days, and schools and institutions were left in ruins. But rather than remain trapped in bitterness, the people of Rwanda chose the harder path of forgiveness. Because of that choice, the country has been transformed. Today, Rwanda is one of the safest, and fastest-growing nations in Africa. It's an astonishing story filled with astonishing people—and one our own country could learn so much from.

What do we do to provide comfort?
After Eric's death, we were blessed by numerous family members and friends. Some took care of us in our home by bringing food and helping us clean. My sister-in-law moved in with us for a week and cooked for us. Linden Dungy, a neighboring dentist, shared wisdom from his brother Tony Dungy who had lost his 19-year-old son under very similar circumstances. We met every week for lunch. Others helped me write thank you letters, took us out to basketball games and invited us out to dinner. I can't tell you how grateful I am for these wise and caring friends.

One of the most important things you can say to someone who has suffered a catastrophic loss is that you are glad to see them and sorry for their loss. Give them a hug, help them with errands or food and don't forget about them after the funeral is over.

Frequently I wished that I could just go to sleep for about 10 years, hoping to wake up healed. But it doesn't work like that after a loss. We all have to go through the mourning process. We all have to learn that the life we knew no longer exists and we have to build a new life based upon what we have left. If you are lucky it takes months but, in many cases, it takes years to truly redirect your life to a point where you are no longer overwhelmed by your past or worried about your future.

The key is to live in the moment and experience the simple peace and joys that are right in front of you. I am 68 years old, and I can tell you that the greatest accomplishment in my life outside my faith and my family is that I can now do that. I can 100% enjoy weddings and holidays with my family. I am no longer counting children. I can 100% enjoy spending an entire day with my grandchildren, and I can 100% enjoy giving them back to their parents tired and full of sugar. Life is good again!

In reality, we can't control bad things happening to us, but we can control how hard we work to recover. Grappling with grief takes a lot of hard work and also takes time. In my experience, however, the hard work and the faking of smiles until the real ones emerge, are totally worth it.

How to Help the Bereaved

Grief has no timeline and no rulebook. But your quiet, consistent, and kind presence, can bring deep comfort to those who are hurting. Here's how to help:

Words That Help
- "I'm so sorry for your loss."
- "I miss them too."
- "He/She was so ___. I remember when..."
- "Would you like help with ___?" (Be specific + give a timeline or just take care of a task you can see needs doing)
- I am so glad to see you.

Actions That Help
- Offer hugs and a listening ear.
- Send cards, notes, or small thoughtful gifts.
- Attend the funeral or memorial, if possible.
- Keep showing up: coffee, texts, invitations.

- Follow up on anniversaries, birthdays, and holidays—grief often resurfaces.

Tip: *Put reminders in your calendar to reach out on key dates.*

Supporting a Friend, Coworker, or Colleague
- Grief affects memory, focus, and energy. Be gentle.
- Lighten their load when possible.
- Offer privacy, flexibility, and space to breathe.
- Avoid unsolicited advice—just listen.
- Ask: "What would be helpful today?" If they're unsure, suggest two or three small options.

Special Kinds of Loss
- **Loss of a Child:** Devastating. Say their name. Share a memory. Just be present.
- **Loss of a Parent:** Brings grief and new responsibilities. Ask about them. Offer help with logistics.
- **Loss of a Spouse:** Loneliness + overwhelm. Keep inviting them—even if they say no.
- **Loss of a Sibling:** Especially hard with traumatic deaths. Siblings are often forgotten—ask how they are.
- **Divorce:** A complex loss. Support without judgment. Remind them they are whole.
- **Suicide or Murder:** Traumatic. Avoid details. Offer love, safety, and zero judgment.

Final Thought
Grief doesn't follow a script. The best gift you can give is your steady presence. You don't have to fix it, just don't let them walk through it alone.

Your quiet consistency may mean more than a thousand perfect words.

**Does someone need your presence today?
Reach out. Show up. Stay close.**

Managing Conflict and The Art Peacemaking

Peace cannot be kept by force; it can only be achieved by understanding,
—Albert Einstein

Conflict is one of life's most consistent companions. Whether we're navigating family dynamics, workplace disagreements, or personal misunderstandings, it shows up—sometimes loudly, sometimes quietly, but always with the potential to shape the quality of our relationships.

Learning to manage conflict is essential to building and maintaining healthy connections.

One of the greatest sources of conflict is simply this: we all see the world differently. It's easy to forget that our perceptions differ. Memory and interpretation are shaped by our backgrounds, beliefs, emotional states, and even our birth order. In fact, research consistently shows that two people witnessing the same event will often recall it in drastically different ways. That's not deception—it's neuroscience.

I've seen this play out over and over again, especially when families gather and start reminiscing. One sibling describes a childhood event as an embarrassing disaster. Another remembers it as hilarious and heartwarming. And somehow, each of them ends up as the misunderstood victim. The discomfort of realizing that the world doesn't look the same through other people's eyes can trigger frustration, disbelief, and yes—conflict.

My ability to misunderstand reality became very personal for me in the final years of my husband Jim's life. He was frail, and I did my best to support him. But I often found myself quietly irritated when the TV remote vanished for the third time in a week. I assumed, without saying anything, that Jim had misplaced it. After he passed, the remote continued to disappear. Frequently. I had no one left to blame but myself.

It was a humbling reminder that my assumptions, even the ones I kept to myself, weren't always accurate. And it highlighted one of the most overlooked roots of conflict: misinterpretation. When we jump to conclusions about someone's intentions or actions, we close the door to understanding—and open the door to unnecessary tension.

Of course, there's another powerful force at play in most conflicts: our ego. Simply put, we don't like being wrong. In fact, we're often addicted to being right. That desire to defend our perspective—no matter the cost—can be so strong that it blinds us to the truth right in front of us. It can also prevent us from hearing the very thing that might lead to healing.

Another ego-related issue is how easily we become offended when someone challenges us. Our brains, in their effort to protect us, flip into survival mode. The amygdala, responsible for our fight, flight, or freeze response, kicks into gear—not because we're under physical threat, but because we *feel* emotionally threatened. That survival instinct, and the accompanying urge to fight or run away, while helpful in prehistoric times, is less useful when we're discussing parenting styles or dividing holiday responsibilities.

I experienced the impact of emotional reactivity firsthand during my time as a National Spokesperson for the American Dental Association. Interviewers would sometimes ask intentionally provocative questions, hoping for a heated reaction they could exploit. Our training focused on one key idea: ignore the tone, answer the question. Don't let someone else's emotional intensity hijack your response.

Part 2: More Life Skills for Living Well

That learned skill came in handy at home, too, especially when my daughters were teenagers. Like many teens, they were smart, emotional, and knew exactly which buttons to push. They still recall with some frustration how often I stayed calm and composed in the face of their most passionate arguments. (They also remember, with some satisfaction, the times I didn't.) Staying grounded doesn't guarantee conflict will vanish—but it does prevent it from escalating.

One of the most effective habits I've adopted is working toward being "unoffendable." That doesn't mean ignoring hurtful behavior or dismissing important issues. It means refusing to let someone else's tone, attitude, or mistake control my emotional state. It means pausing before reacting. It means calmly choosing resolution over outrage.

As a mediator, I often saw how a single moment of reframing could change the trajectory of an entire conversation. One person would be locked in on how wrong or unreasonable the other person was—until we shifted the focus from the person to the problem. Instead of, "You're impossible to work with," we'd ask, "What's standing in the way of us finding a solution to this problem?" That shift opened space for collaboration instead of combat.

It's also worth noting that not all conflict is bad. When handled well, it can lead to better understanding, creativity, and stronger relationships. But that only happens when we approach conflict with humility and intention—not when we weaponize our opinions or let our emotions run wild.

And when we *do* mess up—and we will—the best path forward is a sincere apology. A good apology doesn't just say "I'm sorry." According to Psychology Today a good apology includes:

1. **Acknowledgment** – Clearly name what you did. "I shouldn't have spoken to you that way."

2. **Empathy and Remorse** – Let the other person know you understand how your actions affected them. "I can see how that hurt you. I'd feel the same way."
3. **Restitution** – Offer a plan to make it right and avoid repeating the behavior. "I'll work on speaking more respectfully, even when I'm frustrated."

Apologizing well takes courage, but it also builds credibility and trust. It tells the other person: I value our relationship more than I value being right.

The same is true for forgiveness. When we choose to forgive, we are choosing freedom—not necessarily for the other person, but for ourselves. Forgiveness doesn't mean forgetting or excusing harm. It means acknowledging the hurt and choosing to release its hold on us. It clears a path for peace—not perfection, but peace.

Conflict is never comfortable, but it doesn't have to be destructive. The goal is not to eliminate disagreements, but to navigate them. That means listening well, speaking carefully, and leaving room for the possibility that we may not see everything clearly.

So, the next time you find yourself in a disagreement, ask yourself: Am I open to seeing another perspective? Can I calm my initial reaction before responding? And if the remote goes missing—maybe check the cushions before blaming someone else.

Top Ten Tips for Managing Conflict

1. Tame the Ego
Your ego wants to be right. Your relationships want you to be kind. Guess which one lasts longer? Approaching conflict with humility instead of pride opens the door to real resolution—and a lot less drama.

2. Build (and Rebuild) Trust

Trust is earned in drops and lost in buckets. Be honest, consistent, and follow through on what you say. Trust makes conflict feel like a challenge to solve, not a threat to survive.

3. Focus on the Issue, Not the Individual

When conflict gets personal, clarity goes out the window. Target the problem, not the person. Instead of "You're impossible," try "We seem to be stuck—how can we move forward?"

4. Seek to Understand

It's amazing what happens when we stop arguing and start asking, "Help me understand where you're coming from." Curiosity is disarming—and often more persuasive than proving your point.

5. Listen Like It's Your Superpower

Most people don't listen to understand—they listen to reload. Be the exception. Practice active listening: stay present, paraphrase, nod (genuinely). It shows respect, and that alone can lower defenses.

6. Don't Assign Blame or Assume Motives

You are not a mind reader. (Even if you're convinced you're right.) Ask before you assume. And remember, blame fuels conflict—compassion calms it.

7. Anchor to Common Ground

Find something—*anything*—you both agree on, and keep circling back to it. "We both want this to work" is a strong starting place. When the conversation drifts off course (and it will), gently redirect.

8. Show Empathy—Even When It's Hard

Especially when it's hard. Empathy isn't agreement; it's

connection. A simple "That sounds frustrating" can turn tension into trust and shift the tone of the entire conversation.

9. Apologize Without the Asterisk
Skip the "I'm sorry if..." or "I'm sorry but..." Just own it. Remember a genuine apology includes three parts: acknowledge the mistake, express empathy, and offer restitution. Forgiveness is powerful, and yes—it earns you bonus maturity points.

10. Forgive—For Real
Forgiveness is about setting yourself free. Holding onto resentment is like drinking poison and hoping the other person gets sick. Let it go. Move forward.

The world doesn't need more people who win arguments. It needs more people willing to heal them. Be that person. Today.

Part 2: More Life Skills for Living Well

I Can Do It Myself...Until I Can't

Why Independence Still Matters

Growing older is a delicate dance between holding on and letting go, it's a struggle between the fierce desire for independence and the undeniable realities of aging. For many older adults, daily life becomes a balancing act, where asking for help feels like surrender, and maintaining autonomy means everything.

When you do things for yourself, whether it's brushing your own hair, paying your bills, or figuring out how to FaceTime the grandkids—you're reinforcing a deep truth: you're still here.

That matters for your health. Studies show that older adults who maintain a sense of control over their lives live longer, get fewer chronic illnesses, and report greater happiness.

Independence includes not only physical self-reliance but emotional and intellectual autonomy as well. It's choosing what you wear, how you vote, and what books you read. It's also about dignity and being able to choose your own path, manage your own money, prepare your own meals, and live in your own home—even if it's a downsized version with grab bars and a talking thermostat.

My Mayo Moment

My own independence was first challenged in 2010. My doctor at the Mayo Clinic sat me down and delivered the blow: due to nerve damage in my "drilling fingers," my clinical career in dentistry was over. Just like that, the career I had loved for decades—and the primary source of income for our family—was gone. My husband Jim was still recovering from liver cancer and a transplant, and we were both staggering under the weight of grief after losing our son the year before. The pit we were in was deep, and dark.

My body decided to stage a full-blown rebellion. Arthritis torched every joint. The spinal defects from Thalidomide—my unwanted birthright—had finally caught up with me. My back and hips screamed constantly, making even the simplest tasks difficult. So, I began treatment at the Mayo Clinic and was enrolled in their renowned pain rehabilitation program.

This program was intense and holistic. It didn't just focus on medication; it focused on movement, mindset, and mobilizing caregivers. In fact, it required your primary support person to attend with you. I was hopeful. Maybe Jim would finally see how hard this was for me—how deep the pain went and how badly I needed help.

Then came the moment. An educator posed a question to the caregivers: *"If your loved one is sitting next to you on the couch and asks for a glass of water, do you go get it—or ask them to get it themselves?"*

I leaned forward, eager to hear what I knew would be the right answer: *"Of course you get the water! Don't you see how much pain we're in?"*

But then—WHAM. The instructor looked around the room and calmly said, *"You ask them to get it themselves—if they are physically capable, even if it hurts."*

Wait... what?

What about compassion? What about supporting each other? What about our suffering?

Then came the wisdom I didn't want to hear but desperately needed: *The greatest pain isn't the ache in your joints. It's the loss of independence. The fastest road to helplessness is paved with too much help.*

The bigger pain, the educator explained would be for us to lose our independence completely, which would likely happen if we didn't start moving and learn to take care of ourselves. That was not the answer I wanted, but it was the answer I needed. Studies show that the more we move, the better we feel and the healthier we become.

So, I got off the couch.

It hurt like hell at first. But I moved. And then I moved some more. I took charge of my pain before it took charge of me. Managing pain was, and still is, a dance. Every time you choose to stand up when it's easier to sit, every time you get your own coffee in the morning or struggle with your walker in the grocery store rather than ordering delivery, you're choosing to stay in the game.

And if you ever find yourself sitting on a couch, aching, and unsure if you should get up—let me lovingly tell you: Get the water. Your future self will thank you.

The Dependency Dance

A major complication of modern living and increasing life expectancies is that most of us will enter a time when our independence is challenged. Some of us believe that it is the responsibility of our children to take care of us, some of us don't, but most of us will face the time when we need help. One of the best things we can do is to talk to our family before we need help and come up with a plan for the future. In doing so, we can align the expectations of both parties.

One of our first challenges is to understand when we need help. Asking for it too early can cause resentment from our caregivers and asking for it too late can limit our options, or result in catastrophic accidents.

It's easy to cross the line from graciously accepting help to expecting it... and then, worse—demanding it. Especially when we're tired, frustrated, or aching in places we didn't even know we had.

Just because someone loves us doesn't mean they're supposed to be our full-time unpaid assistant.

Caregivers—whether they're adult children, spouses, neighbors, or professional aides—deserve our respect, our boundaries, and our deepest gratitude. It's important to understand how to receive help well without draining the very people who are pouring love into our lives. Because asking for help is wise. Expecting others to read our minds and sacrifice their own lives to keep ours running? Not so much.

The Caregiver Conundrum
Caregivers are saints with coffee stains.

They juggle jobs, kids, doctor's appointments, medication schedules, and emotional landmines with grace and (hopefully) a sense of humor. Many are members of the Sandwich Generation—squeezed between raising children and caring for aging parents, while trying not to completely lose themselves in the process.

And while it may look like they've got it all together, beneath that calm exterior is often a stressed-out soul.

None of us sets out to take our caregivers for granted. It happens gradually.

We start innocently enough. "Would you mind grabbing me some milk?" becomes "And eggs, and bread, and oh, can you return these shoes to that store I forgot the name of, and also call my insurance company while you're at it?"

It's a form of entitlement creep—the slow shift from appreciation to assumption. From "thank you so much" to "you should help me."

But no one owes us that kind of sacrifice, not even our kids.

If we're not careful, we end up not only burning out our caregivers but also damaging the very relationships we cherish most.

Caregivers need us to let them have boundaries. That might mean they can't help today. That might mean they ask you to hire a cleaning service, use a grocery delivery app, or (gasp) wait an extra day for a ride.

It might hurt your pride. But giving them permission to say "no" is one of the greatest gifts you can give them.

Know When to Wave the White Flag

On the other hand, it is also important to know when it is time to ask for help.

My husband Jim struggled with this. He suffered numerous falls yet was in denial. He refused to use his wheelchair and eventually fell and broke his shoulder setting off one hospitalization after the other. He passed away two months later. There is a difference between independence and denial. The key to graceful aging isn't clinging to independence like it's a life raft—it's learning how to recognize when you really do need help and not being afraid to ask for it. An important strength we can develop in this season of life is flexibility. The ability to say, "I used to do it all myself. But now, I need to share the load."

Letting others help when you can't help yourself can be a gift to them, too. It gives your adult children a chance to serve you with the same tenderness you once gave them. It deepens relationships. It builds trust. It creates a bridge between generations that says, "We're in this together."

We need to respect our caregivers and try—really try—before we ask. Their gift to us is their presence and help when we really need them

Set Strong Boundaries

As we get older, we start to see more clearly who truly loves and values us—not for what we can do, but simply for who we are. It's easy to get caught up in giving and giving, hoping for appreciation or love in return, but the truth is, love doesn't have to be earned or begged for. Real love shows up with respect, gratitude, and kindness. It doesn't come with conditions or only appear when someone needs something. That's why setting boundaries is so important. It helps protect your peace and keeps your energy from being drained by people who take more than they give.

We all deserve to be surrounded by people who lift us up and bring joy into our lives. Not everyone will understand your boundaries—and that's okay. Sometimes the people who push back the most are the ones who were benefiting from you not having any. But protecting your peace isn't selfish; it's healthy. Let go of the guilt, and let go of anyone who makes you feel like your worth is tied to how much you do for them. Keep close the ones who truly see you, love you, and support your growth. Peace, joy, and genuine connection are worth more than approval or proximity—choose them every time.

How to Accept Help Without Becoming a Burden

Here are some practical ways to get what you need without taking more than you should:

1. Do What You Still Can Do
If you can make your own sandwich, do it. If you can fold your own laundry, fold away. Doing things for yourself is respectful and it keeps you mentally and physically stronger.

2. Bundle Your Requests
Instead of peppering your caregiver with five calls a day, keep a list. Be strategic. Say: "Hey, when you're coming over Tuesday, could we do these three things together?" Respect their time like you would a professional.

3. Say Thank You (Often and Creatively)

Gratitude goes a long way. Write a thank-you note. Leave a voicemail that says, "You're the best part of my week." Or better yet, give them time back—babysit their kid, send them on a coffee break, or just not ask for anything today.

4. Ask, Don't Assume

"Could you help with this?" leaves room for a yes or no. "I need you to come right now" does not. When you ask, you give them a choice. That's empowering.

5. Share Your Appreciation Publicly

Brag about your caregiver. Brag to your friends, on Facebook, at church, to anyone who will listen. "My son is amazing. He's juggling so much, and I'm so proud of him." Let them overhear it. It matters.

6. Use Support Services When Possible

There's no shame in hiring a little help. If your budget allows, use it to lighten the load on your family. A house cleaner once a month. A rideshare app for errands. A meal delivery service. Think of it as love insurance

7. Don't Weaponize Guilt

Please, don't say, "Well, I wiped your butt when you were a baby" every time they hesitate to do something. Yes, you did. But that was your job. Now they have jobs, kids, spouses, deadlines, dental appointments, and knee pain of their own.

Ten Signs You're Ready for the Gentle Descent: Big House → Cozy Place → Someone Else Cooks

1. **Stairs are a challenge, not a workout.**
   If navigating your own home feels risky or exhausting, it's time to rethink your space.
2. **You're living in 10% of your house.**
   If the guest room, basement, and upstairs have become ghost towns, you may not need all that square footage.
3. **The loneliness is louder than the television.**
   When social isolation becomes the norm, a supportive community can be a life-giving change.
4. **You've had a fall-or a close call.**
   If your balance or mobility is changing, safety should take priority before an accident forces the issue.
5. **You're skipping meals or forgetting medication.**
   When daily self-care starts slipping, it's time to get help with structure and support.
6. **Home maintenance feels like a full-time job.**
   If mowing, shoveling, or fixing things is causing stress, downsizing can bring relief.
7. **Driving no longer feels safe or fun.**
   If you're avoiding errands or driving feels overwhelming, a place with provided transportation can help.
8. **Health needs are increasing.**
   Frequent medical appointments, new medications, or chronic conditions may require closer care.
9. **Your kids are gently (or not-so-gently) nudging you.**
   If loved ones express concern, it's worth listening-even if it's hard to hear.
10. **You want peace of mind, not just independence.**
    Transitioning before a crisis allows you to choose your next chapter with confidence-not in panic.

How to Get Along with Your Adult Children Without Really Trying (and Vice Versa)

I will leave the world a better place, because of my children and their children, they are my most beautiful and treasured legacy. If I do nothing else, I did that.
—Anonymous

Research tells us that the best predictor of happiness in life is the quality of the relationships you maintain. There is no relationship that shifts over time and requires more adaptation than the relationships between parent and child. In a typical lifetime, you give birth to them, and they bury you. And there comes a moment when you look across the table at your adult child—the one you bathed, bribed with Sour Patch Kids, and threatened with "the look"—and you realize you're no longer the manager of their life. You have been demoted to the advisory board with no voting rights.

At the same time, there's a moment when your adult child—now sporting definitive opinions, career stress, and maybe a piercing you pretend not to notice—looks back at you and wonders, "How do I love this person...when they think privacy is just a phase I will grow out of?

Welcome to the beautifully complicated dance between parents and adult children. It is sacred. It is stretching. It's kind of like herding cats... blindfolded... during a windstorm. But it is also one of the most life-giving relationships you will ever build—*if* you're willing to learn a few new steps along the way.

From the Parent's View: "I gave birth to you!"
Let's just say it—raising a human being is not for the faint of heart. You fed them, clothed them, taught them not to call 911 unless it was a real emergency. Suddenly, you're the one who doesn't understand

the joke, and they're not explaining it. It's jarring.

But here's the truth: your job as a parent hasn't ended, it has *evolved*. You are no longer the captain of the ship. But you can guide. You can help. You can stay steady while they navigate. You also need to back off when necessary and realize that life comes in seasons, whether you like the new season or not.

This shift requires enormous humility. You don't get to dictate curfews or take the car away anymore. What you do get to offer is something even more powerful—unconditional love, safe space, and the wisdom of someone who has survived —a lot.

We have to remember that when our adult child makes their own choices or doesn't include us in every gathering, it's not a rejection—it's part of them building their own life. They are becoming their own person. Isn't that what we raised them for?

So, bite your tongue sometimes. OK, bite your tongue a *lot*. Cheer their wins. And when they fail, don't say, "I told you so." Just say, "I'm here. Always." And remember, independence isn't distance, it's development.

From the Adult Child's View: "Let Me Find My Own Way!"

Dear grown-up kids (yes, I'm talking to you—even if you're 47), your parents are doing their best. They didn't get a handbook when they brought you home, just sleep deprivation and a baby who thought 3AM was party time.

Your parents are human beings who worry about you. They miss being needed. They often feel left behind in a world that now frequently sidelines them.

They still love you with the kind of fierce, stubborn love that keeps 40-year-old school projects in boxes and tears up at old voicemail messages. But they are also still learning. Give them grace.

Your parents may never understand your politics, taste in music or your decision to name your dog after a movie character they never heard of, but they are trying. So, meet them halfway. Let them in. Teach them kindly. And for heaven's sake, answer their text—even if it's just a thumbs-up.

They don't want to control your life; they want to stay a part of it. Invite them in and give them clear instructions. Trust me, they'll appreciate it more than guessing. Don't put this off, the longer you delay setting boundaries, the harder it will be for everyone.

Love That Completes vs Love That Competes

You've seen the research—happy people have strong relationships, and successful kids have more than one loving adult cheering them on. So why, when it comes to grandparents, do some parents treat affection like it's a limited resource to be guarded? Can we call it jealous love or a deep insecurity that sees every other close bond as competition? It's a classic, and unfortunately, it's a tragedy. Because when adults let their pride call the shots, kids are the ones who miss out. And in most cases, the power lies with the parents—who, in a moment of frustration or fear, may slam the door on a relationship their child desperately needs.

Now don't misunderstand me—if Grandma's toxic or Grandpa's a gaslighter, boundaries are necessary. But ask yourself this: Is this boundary about safety or just discomfort about sharing the spotlight?

Giving your child the chance to love more people doesn't mean they'll love you less. In fact, they might grow up with a deeper capacity for love, patience, and wisdom. So maybe it's time to take a breath, drop the tug-of-war rope, and remember: when a child is wrapped in many safe, loving arms, everybody wins.

Estrangement: A Legacy No One Wants

It's a quiet heartbreak that affects more people than we realize—at least one in four adults experience some form of estrangement from a parent. That's not just a statistic; it's millions of untold stories of distance, disappointment, and the deep ache of disconnection in what should be our most foundational relationships.

Cutting ties in one generation often leaves scars in the next. If your family is fractured, start by naming it. Then dig gently for the root causes: miscommunications, unmet needs, or old wounds that never got stitched up right. If you're stuck, consider a mediator or therapist—someone neutral who can help navigate the landmines. Of course, if the relationship involves abuse, manipulation, or harm, protecting yourself may be the healthiest and most courageous choice. Not every relationship can—or should—be repaired.

This is hard work. But you're not alone. Countless families are desperately trying to find their way back to one another. By prioritizing kindness over control, we can give our families something money can't buy: peace, understanding, and lasting love.

The Glue: Humility, Humor, and Honest Conversations

What keeps this whole messy thing called family together is not always shared opinions. It's shared respect.

Parents: Be brave enough to say, "I messed up."

Adult children: Be humble enough to say, "I was too harsh."

Don't play the blame game. Play the *remember-why-we-love-each-other game.*

Create boundaries that protect peace, not punish people. And when conflict happens (because it will), let love interrupt the spiral. Remember, the relationship is more important than being right.

Also, laugh together. Seriously. Nothing heals old wounds like shared laughter over awkward memories or Dad's infamous idiosyncrasies (You know the ones.)

Part 2: More Life Skills for Living Well

What You'll Never Regret

You'll never regret saying, "I love you" more than necessary.

You'll never regret choosing grace over grudges.

You'll never regret pausing an argument to say, "Let's try that again."

You'll never regret sharing the pictures, writing down the stories, the memories, the wisdom—so your children and grandchildren can hold your voice long after you're gone.

And you'll certainly never regret giving each other the gift of presence. Because in the end, it's not about the number of conversations you have. It's about whether those conversations build connections or tear them down.

Legacy Work Begins Here

As someone who works in legacy and grief, I've seen too many families mourn with unfinished business. Too many hearts weighed down with "I wish I had said..." or "I wish we'd had more time."

Let's not wait for crisis or funerals to say the good stuff. Say it now. While they're alive. While you're annoyed. While you're still figuring it out.

Make peace. Keep peace. Pass on peace.

Because the legacy you're building—whether you know it or not—is not about achievements or inheritance. It's about how well you loved your people. Loving well means knowing when to lean in, when to step back, and always choosing the bridge over the battleground.

When 'Stay in Touch' Means Two Very Different Things.

The Ten Commandments for Parents and Their Adult Children

1. Thou shalt not expect thy adult child to answer thy call upon the first ring, nor shalt thou assume they have perished if they reply not within the hour.
2. Adult children, thou shalt not leave thy laundry, thy pets, or thy children at thy parents' house, then depart with haste and without explanation.
3. Parents, thou shalt not show up unannounced. Behold, even the Lord knocketh before entering.
4. Adult child, thou shalt honor thy father and thy mother, even if they useth emojis strangely and misquoteth The Google.
5. Thou shalt not keep score of who calleth whom last. Love seeketh not its own, nor doth it keep a spreadsheet.
6. Adult child, thou shalt accept thy parents' quirks as a burnt offering of love—yea, even if they re-use plastic bags and speaketh of weather as if it were breaking news.
7. Parents, thou shalt accept that thy child knoweth not how to write a check, dial a landline, or use the fax machine—these mysteries are hidden from them.
8. Thou shalt not withhold forgiveness, even when thy adult child rolleth their eyes, or when thy parent asketh again, "What is TikTok, and why doth it?"
9. And lo, when disagreements cometh, thou shalt remember: love never faileth, but passive-aggressive comments often doth. Choose ye this day the way of peace.
10. Above all these, thou shalt put on love, and also patience, long-suffering, and a sense of humor, for family is messy and miraculous, and thou art stuck with one another forever.

Go call your kids (or your parents) and tell them you love them.

Conquering Loneliness

Loneliness and the feeling of being unwanted is the most terrible poverty.
– Mother Teresa

Eighty percent of women die single. Seven out of ten are widowed. Meanwhile, eighty percent of men die married. The numbers don't lie: women tend to outlive their spouses, and men tend to outlive their independence. Loneliness, however, doesn't discriminate. If you are the one left behind or the one still trying to figure out how to work the washing machine, or change the light bulb, it has a way of creeping in. This chapter dives into the universal ache of loneliness, especially in life's later years—and how we can learn to find purpose and joy and the understanding that we are enough alone.

I knew I'd feel lonely after Jim died. What I didn't anticipate was the depth of that loneliness — how it would settle in like an unexpected and unwelcome houseguest wearing his favorite flannel shirt.

Jim passed away during the COVID pandemic, after a long stretch of hospitalizations where I couldn't even be at his side. I had already experienced a good deal of solitude, both while he was in care and during my own two-week hospital stay at the height of lockdown. It was painful, but bearable — because I still believed I'd see him again.

Then one day, that changed.

The day he died, Jim's sisters kindly offered to stay with me overnight. I almost declined. I thought, I'll be fine. I'm strong. But once the house emptied and the sun began to set, I felt the first wave of something far heavier than solitude. It wasn't just quiet. It was the aching silence of a world without him. And I was suddenly, deeply grateful I wasn't alone.

What Loneliness Really Feels Like
Loneliness after the death of a spouse isn't just about missing conversation or companionship. It's the absence of your person — the one who knew your stories, your quirks, your rhythms. It's the sudden disappearance of your shared history, the daily check-ins, the unspoken understandings.

For years, my purpose revolved around Jim's care. Suddenly, there was no one to look after, and no one to look after me. No one asking what we were having for dinner. No one caring if I got home safely. My home was the same. But my life was not.

You Can't Erase Loneliness — But You Can Push Back
You can't fill the void left by someone you love. But you can take steps to soften the edges of grief and restore connection in your life.

For me, it took time — and intentional effort. I reached out to friends, stayed active, and said yes to just about any invitation that came my way. I made a habit of visiting my kids and grandkids, often bringing gifts (bribery works with kids). I joined a widow's support group, explored new interests, and slowly found myself again.

Loneliness doesn't disappear by itself, and healing doesn't happen in isolation. We need people. Not perfect ones — just present ones. Loneliness loses power the moment we say, "I need you," and someone shows up. Rebuilding takes guts. But it's the only road to life again.

You're Not Alone — In Feeling Alone
In fact, the U.S. Surgeon General recently issued an advisory on loneliness, calling it a public health crisis. That means millions of people are quietly struggling with the same sense of disconnection. It's not just you — and it's not your fault.

When personal grief meets a widespread epidemic of social isolation, the effects can be profound. But the truth is: we're wired for connection. And even in loss, we can find new ways to belong.

Grief or Depression? It's Important to Know the Difference

Grief is a natural response to profound loss. But over time, if those feelings don't begin to ease — or if they intensify — it may signal the onset of depression, which is a clinical condition requiring care and support.

This issue is deeply personal to me as I faced a change in my purpose, identity and deep loneliness after all of my losses. After our son's death, I sought emotional help. Jim didn't. He believed asking for support was a sign of weakness — something to "tough out."

His body disagreed. Two years after Eric's death, Jim required emergency heart surgery. Ten years later, he died of congestive heart failure. I will always believe his death was hastened by unresolved grief and untreated depression. The phrase "a broken heart" may be poetic, but it can also be heartbreakingly real.

Know the Signs of Depression

It's not always easy to distinguish grief from depression, but here are some signs to watch for:

- Persistent feelings of sadness, emptiness, or hopelessness
- Loss of interest in things once enjoyed
- Changes in appetite or sleep (either too much or too little)
- Difficulty concentrating or making decisions
- Physical aches and pains without a clear cause
- Ongoing fatigue or restlessness
- Thoughts of self-harm or suicide

If these symptoms resonate with you, please seek help. Depression is not a moral failing or a personal flaw. It's a medical condition — and one that is treatable.

There is no shame in asking for support. In fact, it's an act of courage.

If you're reading this and feeling unseen, I want you to know: you matter. Your story, your strength, and your struggle all matter.

You may have lost the person who knew you best, but that doesn't mean your life has lost its meaning. There are still moments of joy to be found, relationships to be built, and new purpose waiting to unfold.

You are not invisible. And you are not alone.

The grief pit is a terrible place to live. Please keep up the fight to escape it and if you are not making progress, seek help.

Bend, Don't Break: The Power of Resilience

The greatest glory in living lies not in never falling, but in rising every time we fall.
—Nelson Mandela.

Wouldn't it be great if life were easy—if we could get through it without sorrow, pain, death, or disappointment? Just one smooth road paved with joy, sunshine, and perfectly ripe avocados. But the reality is this: life is not easy. Life is hard.

The older you get, the more loss you suffer. Think about it—either you die young, or you watch the people you love die around you. There's no way to sugarcoat that one. And yet, in one of life's most fascinating paradoxes, older adults—"Perennials," as I like to call us—are among the happiest demographic groups around. Despite our decaying bodies, declining memories, and the fact that we know which funeral homes have the most comfortable seating, we're still smiling.

Why? Because we've learned the power of resilience.

The Science and Soul of Bouncing Back

According to the American Psychological Association, resilience is "the process and outcome of successfully adapting to difficult or challenging life experiences, especially through mental, emotional, and behavioral flexibility." In simpler terms, it's learning to bend so you don't break.

And BBC Science Focus Magazine recently reported that being mentally resilient can reduce your risk of dying within the next ten years by 54%. Fifty four percent! That's enough to make me feel slightly less guilty about skipping my morning workout. (Slightly.)

The truth is, we all face loss—rejection, financial insecurity, betrayal, illness, death. And we don't all respond the same way. Some of us crumble. Some of us claw our way through. And some, eventually, learn how to not just survive, but grow stronger.

Resilience can be taught. It can be modeled. It can even be inherited—not just through our DNA, but through our stories, our habits, and our love.

The Parenting Assignment of a Lifetime

Building resilience in myself and passing those skills on to my children and grandchildren has become deeply personal for me, especially after losing so many family members to suicide. I've seen firsthand what can happen when pain has no outlet and despair feels permanent.

So now, when my grandchildren face disappointments—like not being chosen for a play, losing a game, or watching a close friendship unravel, I don't try to rescue them from it. Instead, I remind them: this is what it means to be human. Failure is not the opposite of success; it's part of it. It's how we grow, how we learn, how we become wise and compassionate and strong.

And when they suffer big losses, like the death of their beloved Pop Pop, I tell them it's okay to cry, okay to miss him, okay to feel it all. But I also remind them that grief is a journey. There are tasks they can do, steps they can take. And someday, they'll be able to carry his memory with joy instead of just sorrow.

In fact, I even talk to them about my own death. I remind them that when the time comes, the best way they can honor me is to lead joyful, useful lives. A few months ago, my nine-year-old granddaughter Heidi asked, with very serious eyes, "Grandma, if you die... can I still go to Disney World?" I told her, "Not only can you go, but I'm also putting aside money in my will to pay for a family trip. Go. Travel. Ride life's rides. Scream with delight. And then live a big, bold, beautiful life."

Why Older Adults Often Excel at Resilience

It's no coincidence that older people tend to be more resilient. We've had more practice.

According to *World Psychiatry*, our response to stress is influenced by our personal history. But everyone—yes, *everyone*—can learn to grow stronger with time. Experience builds our emotional muscles. And faith, perspective, and a sense of humor don't hurt either.

We can train our brains to overcome pain with mindfulness, gratefulness, and a positive mindset. When we practice it ourselves, we're not just helping our own mental and emotional health, we're modeling a roadmap for our children.

And what a gift that is.

Your Legacy of Resilience

Most of us who've lived long enough to know loss also have stories of redemption, recovery, and the quiet triumph of getting out of bed on the worst days. Don't keep those stories to yourself. Share them.

Tell your kids and grandkids about the time you failed and got back up. Let them see that you've made mistakes and learned from them. Teach them to talk to themselves with the same kindness they'd show a dear friend. Teach them that the voice in their head doesn't have to be a critic. It can be a coach.

If you do this—if you build resilience in your children, grandchildren, nieces, nephews, friends— you will prepare them to thrive. You're giving them tools for joy, strength for sorrow, and a legacy they can lean on when you're no longer here.

So don't wait. Start today. Share your stories. Model resilience. Teach them how to bounce—not just back, but forward. Because the greatest inheritance isn't what you leave for them, it's what you leave in them.

Practical Ways to Build Resilience in Children

There are five key ways we can help the next generation grow resilient roots:

1. Let Them Struggle (Just a Bit).
Kids don't learn perseverance if we fix everything for them. Let them wrestle with hard things—spelling words, friendship drama, algebra. Struggle teaches strength.

2. Normalize Disappointment.
Share your own stories of rejection and regret. Let them see that you've failed—and survived. That you've been wrong—and recovered. That you've been heartbroken—and healed.

3. Teach Emotional Literacy.
Help them name their feelings: "You seem angry," or "That must've really hurt." When kids can talk about emotions, they're less likely to be ruled by them.

4. Model Problem-Solving.
I even throw in a little conflict management training when I can. I remind them: Don't take the bait of offense. Focus on the problem, not the person. Let go of the need to be right. Get your ego out of the way and move forward. Honestly, that works for adults, too.

5. Keep It All in Perspective.
Kids are watching how we respond to adversity. Do we spiral into panic, or pause to pray? Do we blame, or do we breathe? Model grace, model perspective, and above all—model hope.

Laughing Through the Aches: A Senior's Guide to Growing Old

You know you're getting old when you stoop to tie your shoelaces and wonder what else you could do while you're down there.
—George Burns

My husband was the 12th of 14 children, and I am the youngest in-law, so I get a heads up on what is coming my way through observing my family. I am the only one left who can drive at night so my value in the family has increased! What I have learned is that we need to keep our spirits high and laugh with each other, even in the difficult times. The family that started out with 14 are now down to 10. We are losing our independence and life is changing. In some cases, our children have become our caretakers.

Aging is a strange, bittersweet journey. It sneaks up on you. One day, you look in the mirror and see a face that has lived—a face marked by love, loss, and laugh lines. They are called the golden years, but some days, they feel more like the "rusty years," where everything creaks, groans, and complains.

Yet, despite the aches, the forgetfulness, and a large collection of prescription bottles that we keep in a zip lock bag, there is something undeniably beautiful about growing old. It's the wisdom of experience, the depth of love shared over decades, and the realization that life—though fragile—is still worth living fully, even if it looks very different than it once did. There is something undeniably hilarious about growing old. No matter how much we exercise or how healthy our diet is we will still age. So, why not look ageing in the face and just laugh. Laughter beats crying any day!

The Perils of a Body That Betrays You

Remember when you could sleep in any position and wake up feeling fine? Ah, the good old days. Now, if you sleep at the wrong angle, your neck is out of commission for a week. You sneeze too hard, and suddenly your lower back files for early retirement. And let's not even talk about the grand adventure of getting up from the couch—because standing now comes with its own sound effects.

But here's the secret: instead of fighting your body, negotiate with it. Stretch in the morning, move often, and, if necessary, bribe your joints with heating pads and an extra scoop of ice cream. And always, always have a comfy chair nearby—because sitting is one of life's greatest luxuries after 65.

Where Are My Glasses? Oh... On My Face.

Memory loss is nature's way of keeping life exciting. You walk into a room with confidence, only to forget why you're there. You tell the same joke to the same person multiple times, and the best part? They forget they've heard it before, so you both laugh like it's the first time. It's like having a built-in rerun of your best material! And for your children, who *will* tell you that you are repeating yourself, you will give them lots of material to use when they write your eulogy.

But let's be real—the real danger isn't forgetting names or why you came into a room. The real horror is forgetting where you put something important, like your phone, keys, or dignity.

If you lose your glasses, check your head first. If you lose your phone, call it from your landline... if you still have one. And if you lose your sanity, just blame it on the grandkids.

For a growing number of us, memory loss might signal the onset of dementia. That's a scary thought. If you are concerned, get to your doctor. There are some treatments that may slow the disease down if you get help early. And researchers are always working on a cure.

However, if you are diagnosed with any decline in your cognitive ability, it is even more important to do your legacy work now. Tell the story of who you are while you can still remember and leave as many positive memories as possible for your loved ones now.

Doctor's Appointments: The New Social Calendar

There was a time when your week was filled with fun outings, travel plans, and dinner dates. Now? Your schedule revolves around doctor's appointments, lab work, and trips to the pharmacy. You know you're getting old when the receptionist at your doctor's office greets you by name and asks about your grandkids before you even check in.

The best way to handle this medical merry-go-round? Turn it into a competition. Compare lab results with your friends. Celebrate the victories—"My cholesterol is lower than yours!"—and laugh at the absurdities, like when they ask you to fill out paperwork on a clipboard with font so small you need a magnifying glass (which, naturally, you can't find).

And let's not forget the joys of "surprise ailments." You go in for a routine check-up, and suddenly, the doctor finds something new to keep an eye on. At this point, your body is like an old car—there's always something making a weird noise, and the warranty expired decades ago.

But medical issues, like a declining brain, can also signal a time when you need to prepare to make changes in your life. Don't put off downsizing until it is too late. Plan ahead. Make changes and get help when you need it.

Fashion Choices: Comfort Over Style

At some point, you stop caring about fashion trends. High heels? Please. If it doesn't have arch support, it's dead to you. If there's one thing aging teaches you, it's that comfort is king. You've earned the right to wear whatever you want. Elastic waistbands? Yes. Fuzzy slippers in the grocery store? Why not? A bathrobe at noon? Sounds like a perfect day.

Technology: Designed to Confuse You
Why does everything have so many buttons now? The TV remote looks like it could launch a spaceship. Your phone does things you never asked it to do. And what about those apps—why do you need an app for everything? What happened to just picking up the phone and talking to people?

The key to surviving technology in old age is to find a young person to explain it all to you. Grandkids are especially useful for this, though they will roll their eyes at you and sigh dramatically before helping. If all else fails, just keep hitting buttons until something works. (Disclaimer: This approach is not recommended for microwaves, bank accounts, or anything with the words "factory reset.")

The Perks of Aging (Yes, There Are Some!)
Sure, growing old comes with its challenges, but let's focus on the perks. Senior discounts? Yes, please. No one expects you to lift heavy things? Fantastic. You can get away with saying whatever's on your mind because "Oh, they're just old"? Priceless.

Plus, there's a certain freedom that comes with age. You no longer care what people think. You can dance at weddings like nobody's watching (because honestly, no one is). You say what you mean, because life's too short for nonsense. And best of all, you can take a nap whenever you want—no permission needed.

Chronic Pain: Living Proof That Growing Older Isn't for Sissies
Chronic pain has been my close companion for 20 years. I just wish it would take a vacation. Permanently. Suddenly the very vessel that carried me all my life has turned on me. Arthritis, neck pain, back pain, joint pain, auto-immune disease...the list is endless. Sometimes

it feels that everything hurts. Thank goodness today we can get treatment and, sometimes, it helps. I have been fortunate. After injections, a new hip, a couple of back surgeries, foot surgeries, saying goodbye to my gall bladder and appropriate medications, I can function. Some of my friends, however, are not so lucky.

Chronic pain doesn't always show on the outside, but it changes everything on the inside—how you move, how you plan, how you interact. You try to ignore it, you try to reason with it, you even threaten it with yoga, but it just settles in with a smug little grin. There's nothing like a stabbing pain in your hip to remind you that gravity is, in fact, winning. But you keep going, maybe slower, maybe with a limp and a heating pad in your purse—but you go.

The secret is to persevere. At the Mayo Clinic Pain Rehab program I learned the hard lesson that if you don't fight chronic pain by continuing to do everything you can, you will lose the ability to do anything. Learn to celebrate the small victories: getting out of bed in the morning without cursing, finding pants that don't make your joints protest, and reaching out to friends. Become a resilience expert, a master of pacing, and a connoisseur of over-the-counter creams. You can cry about the pain or laugh at the absurdity of it—either way, you're releasing something that needs to come out. Pain may have changed your pace, but it hasn't stolen your purpose. Keep walking toward joy, even if it's one slow, stubborn step at a time.

Final Thoughts: Laugh While You Can

I discovered the healing power of laughter during some of my darkest days. Years ago, during one of Jim's "close to death" events, his sisters supported me in the most peculiar way. Jim was in rough shape after heart surgery, refusing a face mask meant to help his dangerously low oxygen levels. Frustrated by his logic-defying insistence that he could raise his numbers by watching them—even while napping—I stormed out, muttering, "I'm not going to stand here and watch you die of stubbornness."

When I returned, he was finally masked up. Crisis averted.

Later, his sisters—Judy, Sue, and Lois—showed up cheerful as ever. I, however, was not in the mood for cheer. "Don't make him talk," I pleaded. "He needs to breathe!" Instead of sympathy, Judy looked at me with a grin and said, "Oh, Kim, stop being such a witch." Only she didn't say witch. Her word began with a "B".

Coming from the ultimate church lady who had never scolded me in over forty years, it shocked my system—in the best way. I burst out laughing. So did everyone else. Even Jim. That laughter lifted us. When anxiety crept back in, one of the sisters would whisper "witch," and we'd collapse in giggles. The sacred kind that mixes with tears and somehow holds you up.

Jim had frequent almost dead encounters before he finally passed away. On one occasion when he suffered from septic shock, was in a coma and had just had a heart attack, I was in tears on the phone with Lois, "I am so scared" I said, "I need someone to call me a (w)itch". Lois complied and in another dark time we broke out into sacred laughter.

So yes, I believe in laughter. Especially when it's wrapped in love and delivered by someone who knows when to break the rules to help you breathe.

Aging is inevitable, but misery is optional. The best way to deal with growing old is to laugh at the absurdity of it all. Laugh at your creaky knees, at the fact that you now discuss fiber intake with your friends, and at the realization that you've become your parents.

Life is short, but if you're lucky, it's also long enough to gather some great stories, make some hilarious mistakes, and love deeply. So, embrace the wrinkles, enjoy the naps, and never forget—if you can't remember why you walked into the kitchen, at least grab a cold drink while you're there.

5 Steps to Age with Humor and Grace

1. Embrace the Absurd
Aging is weird—your joints predict the weather, and tying your shoes feels like a workout. Laugh anyway. It helps.

2. Let Go of the Mirror
Your reflection may change, but your joy and stories don't. Treasure the life that brought you here.

3. Keep Your People Close
Aging with grace is a team sport. Stay connected. Laugh often. And yes, let your friends fix your rogue eyebrow pencil.

4. Stay Curious
Try something new. Keep your brain dancing. Curious hearts age better—and laugh more.

5. Leave Love, Not Baggage
Pass down wisdom and laughter, not drama. Forgive freely, hug often, and let kindness be your legacy.

And remember: if you're lucky, you'll get old. Do it boldly. Do it kindly. And never lose your sense of humor—it's the best wrinkle cream on the market.

Success in Retirement: Finding Your Purpose

"The purpose of life is not to be happy, but to be useful, to be honorable, to be compassionate, to have it make some difference that you have lived and lived well."
—Ralph Waldo Emerson.

As we go through life's stages, retirement stands out as a shining star that we aspire to. We crimp, we save, and we frequently picture ourselves in an amazing location having fun 24 hours a day. Research is showing us, however, that for some, fun in the sun gets boring after a while and many of us start looking for more.

Of course, not everyone has the luxury of retiring. For some, financial realities make it necessary to keep working far beyond the traditional retirement age. The dream of endless vacations is simply not feasible for everyone, and that's a truth we need to honor with compassion and respect.

My husband Jim retired from dentistry at 66 and gave up his license because we wanted to travel. And travel we did. We cruised, we toured, we hung out in fabulous places. For about three years we left the Minnesota cold right after Christmas and drove south to our daughter's house in Kansas City. While there we would decide to turn either right and visit the southwest or turn left and visit the southeast. We had fun.

But after a while we both got bored. I was working part time speaking and consulting and I was an avid porcelain painter. But Jim had not developed any hobbies. He missed dentistry and after three years he decided to do the work and get his license back (which, by the way is a lot harder than just keeping it.). He learned the hard way that we need to think twice before giving up our professional licenses!

Once Jim got his license back, he began teaching and he loved it. He loved the structure, he loved the subject, and he loved the students. Jim found his late life purpose and it brought him great joy.

At the same time, I practiced my hobby of painting porcelain and found my tribe in the porcelain painters' guild. When I paint, I lose track of time and space. After Jim died it was great antidote to loneliness. I also found the same peace, happiness and energy when I wrote or developed presentations. For a number of years, I traveled almost every week speaking in dentistry.

After a while, I discovered that my new passion was helping people navigate the 4th quarter of their lives and I became a death doula, wrote books and began speaking about widowhood and building legacy. My current plan now is to continue speaking as long as I am able to travel and then help other people find their purpose in life as a coach. Painting will be my backup until I can no longer hold a brush!

At the same time, I want to be an active part of my grandchildren's lives so I traded our old dream of retiring with Jim in the Northwoods (retiring by myself in the Northwoods would be pretty lonely) to living part time in Minneapolis and part time in Kansas City to be near each set of grandchildren. At this stage in my life this is working out great. I know that as I decline, I will have to simplify and face the next chapter but for now, I am happy.

We all want to believe our lives matter, even after we retire. We all want to believe that we're here for something more than just paying bills. We ache for purpose—a reason to get out of bed.

But what is purpose? Really?

Here's something I've learned the hard way: **Your purpose isn't a destination. It's a direction.** It's not a job title or a five-year plan. It's not something you earn after enough therapy, yoga, or TED Talks.

Your purpose is already inside you, patiently waiting for you to stop long enough to hear it whisper, *"Hey... remember me?"*

The Myth of the One Big Thing

There's a dangerous myth out there that says you only have *one* true purpose in life, and if you don't find it by age 35, you've missed the bus. That's nonsense. (And as someone who has taken quite a few detours in life—some of them scenic, some of them train wrecks—I can assure you the purpose bus has no schedule and lots of stops.)

Your purpose might change as you change. It might look one way when you're raising kids, another way when you're caring for aging parents, and something else entirely when you're staring at the blank page of your future, wondering what story to write next.

I loved the decades I spent as a dentist, helping people smile again. That felt purposeful. But then, life shifted. My hand gave out. My husband died. My children grew. I found myself in a new season with unfamiliar terrain, wondering if purpose had an expiration date. (It doesn't, by the way.)

Purpose doesn't retire. It just reinvents.

Listening to the Longing

Purpose begins with paying attention to the longing inside you—the part that aches for meaning, for connection, for impact. It's that quiet tug when you hear someone's story and think, *I want to help.* Or when you see a problem and feel a spark of, *Maybe I could do something about that.*

You don't need a ten-step plan or a certificate of approval. You need curiosity. You need courage. And you need to love people.

Love is the compass that points you toward purpose. When you love deeply, you want to leave the world better than you found it. You want to build, heal, nurture, create. You want to show up in a way that matters. That's purpose.

Start Where You Are (Seriously, Right Here)
If you're reading this and thinking, okay, but I still don't know what my purpose is, understand: you don't have to know everything. You just have to start where you are.

What breaks your heart?

What brings you joy?

What have you learned the hard way that you wish someone had told you sooner?

Your purpose is probably hiding in plain sight—in the thing you can't *not* care about. In the cause you keep coming back to. In the people who light you up or the problems that won't let you go.

Maybe your purpose is mentoring someone who reminds you of your younger self. Maybe it's finally writing that book, opening that business, starting that nonprofit. Or maybe it's showing up—consistently, kindly, and without applause—for the people in your life who need you.

Big or small, glamorous or gritty—if it's driven by love, it counts.

Detours, Doubts, and Divine Curveballs
Now, let's talk about the mess. Because no journey toward purpose is clean or simple. You will get it wrong. You will doubt yourself. You will try something that flops.

But even the detours teach you something. Even the failures point you forward. Purpose isn't about perfection. It's about showing up anyway.

You may get a divine curveball that knocks you flat—grief, illness, loss, betrayal. And in those seasons, purpose might feel like a cruel joke. But even then, you matter. Even then, you have something to give. Even then, you are not done.

Sometimes, your greatest purpose is born from your deepest pain. The scar becomes a bridge for someone else. The thing you survived becomes the thing you teach, the way you love, the reason you understand.

Permission to Pivot
You are allowed to change your mind. You are allowed to leave what no longer fits and try something new. You are allowed to be a beginner again.

Some people find purpose early. Others stumble into it halfway through a career or after a great loss. There's no shame in the search. In fact, that search—that longing—that reaching for more? That is purpose in motion.

So, if you're in the middle of a pivot, welcome. I've pivoted more times than a Broadway dancer. And every time, I found new grace, new growth, and new love.

Leaving a Trail of Light
In the end, purpose is less about what you do and more about who you become while doing it. It's about the lives you touch, the laughter you share, the kindness you plant in unsuspecting places.

You don't have to change the whole world. Just change your little corner. Make it softer, brighter and more loving. And trust that in doing so, you're living your purpose more fully than you ever imagined.

Don't overthink it. Don't wait for perfect conditions. Start now. Start small. Start scared. Just start.

Because someone out there is waiting for the gift only *you* can give.

Part 2: More Life Skills for Living Well

Ten Clues You Have Found Your Passion for a Purpose

1. You Won't Shut Up About It
Friends fake bathroom breaks when you bring it up *again*. That's passion.

2. You'd Do It for Free
Though let's be honest—you're not opposed to a little Venmo love.

3. You Lose Track of Time
You missed lunch. You don't care.

4. You're Weirdly Protective of It
People who don't get it? You try not to judge. (But you do. A little.)

5. It Keeps Coming Back
You tried quitting it. It didn't quit you.

6. You're Okay Looking Silly
You'll risk failure if it means doing it right.

7. It Feels a Little Scary
Big callings often come with big jitters.

8. You Forget Yourself
Your thighs, your taxes, your to-do list? Gone. You're in the zone.

9. Others Feel the Love
People say things like, "That helped." And you think, *Whoa. I didn't even try that hard.*

10. It Feels Like Home
No pretending. No performance. Just you—doing what you were made to do.

You're Not Dead Yet!

Retirement isn't the end of your story—it's the start of a chapter you finally get to write for yourself. Step into this season with intention, and let your purpose become the legacy that outlives you.

But before you can enjoy this next chapter, you have to protect it. Because sadly, not everyone gets the chance to live their retirement dream—especially if that dream is stolen by a scam.

We all know people who were scammed through bit coins, romance scams, and investments scams which completely changed their ability to retire. And they are NOT alone.

In the chapters ahead, we'll shine a light on the shadowy world of scammers—and how to keep from becoming their next target.

Escape From The Valley Of The Scammed

> *Corruption, embezzlement, fraud, these are all characteristics which exist everywhere. It is regrettably the way human nature functions, whether we like it or not. What successful economies do is keep it to a minimum. No one has ever eliminated any of that stuff.*
> — Alan Greenspan

According to the American Association of Retired People **42% of Americans have experienced fraud and the numbers are growing.** But being the victim of a scam is not just about financial loss; it can leave a gaping emotional wound. It can shake your confidence, steal your sense of peace, and create a quiet shame that keeps you from telling the very people who love you most, or anyone else for that matter. That shame can chip away at your health, your joy and your most cherished relationships.

So why are we talking about scams under a section about life skills? Because scams are part of the world we live in. Smarts and skepticism aren't just helpful—they're essential.

In the senior community, becoming a victim of a scam can even threaten your independence, as family and caregivers lose trust in your ability to manage your own affairs. What begins as financial loss can quietly unravel your autonomy. This can lead to unwanted oversight, loss of decision-making power, or even legal guardianship. Just one convincing lie from a smooth-talking swindler, paired with a moment of misplaced trust, can set off a chain reaction that alters where you live, who holds your checkbook, and how much control you have over your life in the only years you have left.

You're Not Dead Yet!

Before I start this chapter on scamming let me get something out of the way: I believe myself a reasonably intelligent human being. I have a doctorate degree and lots of certifications in life, death, grief and mediation management. I have raised two incredible children and even taught large groups of people how to navigate grief, love, conflict and legacy planning. But do you know what else I have done?

I have been scammed. Yes, scammed. Hoodwinked. Duped. Bamboozled. And not just once, several times. *Oh, the SHAME of it.*

For years, I sat in judgment of the poor souls on talk shows and podcasts who were tricked by promises of love, money, or that magical "once-in-a-lifetime opportunity." I couldn't imagine how anyone could hand over private information—or a good chunk of their savings—to someone who then vanished into thin air. I even, in my less gracious moments, silently judged my own late husband for falling for an investment scam and then a tech support scheme.

Jim, if you're up there, and to everyone else who's been taken in by a scam—I'm sorry. Truly. I get it now. Shame and judgment are the scammer's best friends. They keep us silent, and silence keeps them in business.

According to the Federal Trade Commission, Americans lost over ten billion dollars to scams in 2023. That's billion with a B. The top frauds? Imposters, shady online shopping schemes, romantic fraud, fake negative reviews, fake prizes and lotteries, bogus investments, and phony business and job opportunities. Basically, if it sounds too good to be true, there's probably a scammer behind it—working overtime from a basement with Wi-Fi.

Scammers are like emotional bloodhounds. Are you looking for love? Money? A new job? A great deal? There's an app for that—and they probably built it. They sniff out your soft spots and strike with unnerving precision.

Part 2: More Life Skills for Living Well

In my case, the weak spot was publishing. I self-published a book that actually won a number of awards (yay!), but I had zero experience marketing a book (oops). Turns out, award sites are easy to search, and once my name was on them, the scammers came crawling out of the woodwork.

The first ones promised big results—ads in the New York Times and Los Angeles Times. I call these "semi-scams." Technically, yes, my book appeared in both newspapers. But you needed a magnifying glass to see them. The ads were the size of a postage stamp. Not exactly front-page news.

Then came the bigger promises of traditional publishers, letters of endorsement to literary agents, even book trailers! Again, some work was done, but it was sloppy and ultimately useless. And like a bad infomercial, there was always a next step. One more ad. One more book fair. One more press release. One more fee.

At one point a scammer asked me to send money sooner than I agreed to because his father was dying, and he needed to pay his hospital bill. Ok, you are thinking, she could not possibly fall for that old trick, but I did. This young man had me believing that he was legitimate, he did deliver a few of the things he promised, I sent half of what he asked for but at least it made me suspicious. Finally, when he tried this again by sending me pictures of a medical condition, he claimed to have which again delayed the delivery of the promised project, I asked for my money back through my credit card company.

After that experience, my eyes were opened! I began having fun with the scammers. When a woman called saying she was a noted literary agent interested in my book, I looked her up and a prominent literary agent with her name did exist. But now I was a skeptic, and her voice did not quite match her picture, so I asked the caller to talk to me via Zoom or Facetime. She refused. One scammer down.

A few weeks later I got an amazing letter from an executive from Penguin Random House (PRH) expressing interest in my book, followed by an actual offer of $475,000. WOW. The letter looked official. The executive checked out on the Penguin Random House Website but there was something fishy about the email address. A "representative" even called with the caller ID "Penguin RH". I turned this scam into the Penguin Random House fraud site. That felt good! Another one bites the dust.

Amazingly the Random House offer was followed up a few weeks later with another offer to buy my book from Little Brown Publishing but this time they were only offering between $250,000-$350,000. The scammers just keep on scamming, but the scam value of my book seemed to significantly decline! I let this one go a little further as I was curious about how much money they wanted to charge me to get that big royalty. The answer came quickly. In order to secure a contract, I needed to pay $5000 to clear up any ownership issues. I sent the letter to the fraud department of Little Brown.

Why do intelligent responsible people fall victim to scammers at such an alarming rate?

According to secureworks.com, it's all about emotional triggers. The site lists 7 tools of the tricksters:

1. **Concern** ("Your account's been compromised!")
2. **Love** ("I really care about you. I just need a little help.")
3. **Fear** ("You'll be arrested if you don't pay now!")
4. **Greed** ("You've won a prize!" "I have an investment for you that can't fail.")
5. **Admiration** ("You're such a talented author—we want to represent you.")
6. **Shame** ("Don't tell anyone—it's embarrassing.")
7. **Guilt** ("My dad is dying, and I can't afford the hospital bill." Or "I just gave my kids inheritance to a con artist")

Let's be real—no one wakes up thinking, I'd love to hand over my retirement savings to a stranger today. And yet, millions of smart, capable people do. Not because they're gullible. Because they're human. Scammers don't just target our wallets; they target our hearts, our fears, and our deepest desires. They know how to bypass the brain and go straight for the emotion.

Think about it. When you're grieving, lonely, overwhelmed, or even just hopeful, you're not operating at full capacity. Your radar for "this seems off" gets a little fuzzy. And that's when they strike. They don't lead with logic, they lead with a story. A crisis. A dream (like a traditional publishing contract). A relationship. They mirror back what you most want or most fear, and then they offer the perfect solution... for a price.

And here's the hardest truth: the more self-reliant you are, the more private, the more you pride yourself on good judgment, the more likely you are to feel shame when you're targeted, and the less likely you are to ask for a second opinion. The associated shame of being wrong silences us—and silence is what scammers are counting on. If they can keep you too embarrassed to talk, they can keep running their game.

Armor Up: How to Protect Yourself Before the Hook Is Set

So how do we guard ourselves, not just logically, but emotionally?

First, expect to be targeted. This isn't paranoia—it's preparation. Just like you lock your doors at night, you can mentally prepare to question unexpected emails, texts, or calls that tug at your feelings. Remind yourself: If this really is that important, they won't mind if I take a minute to check it out.

Second, build your "scam squad." Choose one or two trusted people—an adult child, friend, or neighbor that you can check in with when something feels off. Make a pact to talk openly about weird messages, even if it feels silly. One five-minute call can save you thousands of dollars and a mountain of heartache.

Third, create a delay habit. Scammers depend on speed. So, whenever you feel rushed—whether it's a "limited-time offer" or a "critical emergency"—take a breath. Literally. Step away for ten minutes. Sleep on it. The more time you give your rational brain to catch up, the harder it is for emotional manipulation to take hold.

Fourth, reframe the shame. Getting scammed isn't a failure, it's an ambush. It doesn't mean you're weak. It means you were targeted by professionals who are very, very good at what they do. The more we talk about it, the harder we make it for them to win.

Scammers are banking on our silence, our shame, and our speed. But with a little awareness, some emotional backup, and a whole lot of courage to speak up, we can outsmart the con artists and help others do the same.

Four Red Flags That Scream "Scam!"

1. Name-Dropping Fakers: If "the IRS" or "Medicare" suddenly calls you sounding overly friendly or urgently grim, pump the brakes. Scammers love to borrow big names—or make up official-sounding ones—to seem legit. Caller ID? Totally fakeable.

2. The Old Problem-or-Prize Trick: "You owe money!" "There's a virus!" "You've won a cruise!" Whether it's doom or delight, scammers bait you with drama. Real prizes don't come with fees, and the government doesn't break up with you over the phone.

3. Pressure-Cooker Panic: Scammers want you to move fast and think slow. They'll say your bank account is in danger, or the feds are en route—anything to keep you from hanging up and wising up.

4. Weird Ways to Pay: Gift cards, crypto, wire transfers, or mystery checks—if the payment method sounds like something you'd use to bribe a pirate, don't do it.

How to Outsmart a Scam:
1. Block the junk calls and sketchy texts.
2. Never cough up personal info to surprise callers, no matter how convincing they sound.
3. Don't click suspicious links—go straight to the real website instead.
4. Real businesses don't rush or threaten. Scammers do.
5. Got a weird request? Phone a friend before you do anything else.

When in doubt? Pause, protect, and pass it by.

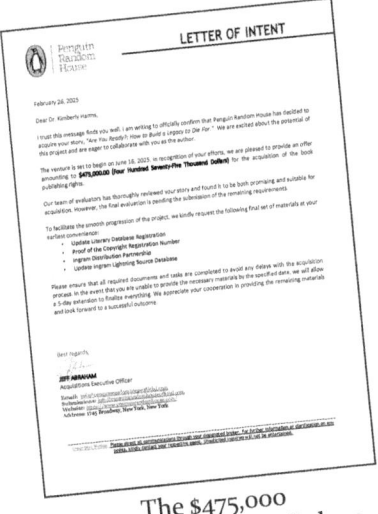

The $475,000 Penguin's Delusion Deluxe Package

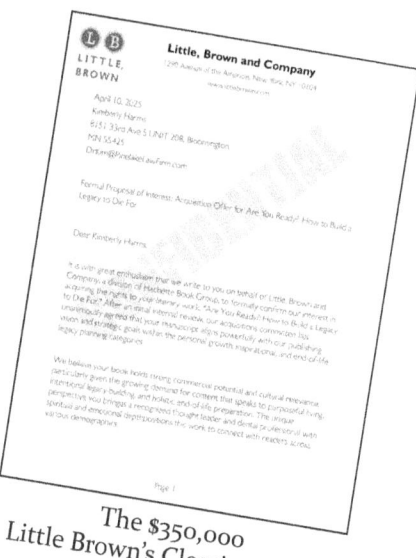

The $350,000 Little Brown's Clearing House of Broken Dreams

Just as scammers can steal your identity, they can also impersonate government agencies, celebrities, romantic interests, reputable investment firms, and even well-known publishers. Before sharing any personal information, passwords, or money, always verify their identity by contacting them directly through their official public channels.

KATHY DEMPSEY

Hey, WAIT KIM! I have to share my scam story!!!

They Didn't Just Steal my Data — They Highjacked My Life!

I had just finished a powerful keynote for the South Carolina Healthcare Association. The crowd was energized. I felt alive, aligned, and on purpose. I grabbed my bags and headed to the airport, feeling like I was exactly where I was supposed to be.

My flight to Charlotte was on time, but once I landed, everything started to unravel.

The connecting flight to Phoenix was delayed three hours. Frustrated, I wheeled my bags through the concourse and found a restaurant to settle in, grab a bite, and get some work done. I noticed my phone was low—20%. I pulled out my charging cord and plugged it into the convenient USB port right at my table.

Three hours later, I boarded, flew home, and thought nothing more of it.

Until a few days later.

That's when I got the first notification: "Your Facebook account has been disabled due to a violation of community standards."

What? I hadn't posted anything. I logged in—nothing. Gone. My personal page. My business page. All of it—shut down. Permanently.

Then things spiraled.

My website went dark. My business email stopped working. My credit cards started flagging thousands of dollars in fraudulent charges—computers, electronics, and equipment being delivered to a fake Scottsdale address under my name.

I called the police, the FTC, credit bureaus, banks, Facebook, you name it. I was told hackers had likely installed a skimming device on that airport charging station. While I was powering up my phone, they were downloading everything—contacts, passwords, payment methods, sensitive personal data.

They accessed my 23,000-person email database and shut it down. They changed my billing address, my birthdate, even my Social Security number, which showed up wrong on my credit report. I had to physically go to the Social Security office and wait for hours just to prove who I was.

They didn't just steal my identity—they stole my business, my momentum, and for a while, my sense of security.

I was spending 5–6 hours a day trying to put the pieces back together. Every day was a new fire to put out. I couldn't work. I couldn't breathe. I was living in crisis mode.

That charging port seemed so harmless. But in under five minutes, it became the open door that nearly shut down everything I had built. Let my story be your wake-up call: identity theft can happen to anyone, at any time, in ways you never see coming. It doesn't care how smart you are, how careful you've been, or where you live.

We like to believe we're safe—especially in "nice" neighborhoods, behind gates, or with fancy security systems. But that's a **false illusion**. I live in a gated community in Scottsdale, Arizona. Just this week, a man was arrested who had been hiding out in my complex for over two years. He was on the run after being convicted in California for a $50 million fraud scheme targeting investors.

Safety isn't about gates or good intentions—it's about awareness.

Power up your awareness, before someone else powers down your life.

What You Can Do to Protect Yourself

- **Avoid public USB charging stations.** Instead, carry a portable battery pack for travel days. It's safer, more secure, and gives you power without the risk.
- **Enable two-factor authentication (2FA) on all major accounts**—especially email, social media, banking, and payment apps.
- **Use strong, unique passwords for every account.** A password manager can keep them secure and make your life easier.
- **Regularly back up your data**—especially contacts, financial records, email lists, and personal files. Don't rely on just one method. Use multiple backup locations: an external hard drive, a secure cloud service, and even a second physical drive stored separately. For critical data, consider 3-4 backup sources to protect against theft, loss, or system failure.
- **Be alert for fake phone calls.** Scammers are getting smarter. They can make it look like your bank or credit card company is calling.

  Tip: Never give personal information on an incoming call. Hang up and call the company directly using the number on the back of your card.

- **Watch for email and text scams using real company logos.** These fake messages often claim you've won something, your account is locked, or you need to "verify" info.

  Tip: Don't click. Go directly to the website yourself.

Part 2: More Life Skills for Living Well

- **Freeze your credit if you suspect any suspicious activity.** Contact Experian, Equifax, and TransUnion individually.
- **Set up transaction alerts through your bank and credit cards.** The sooner you catch fraud, the easier it is to stop.
- **Stay informed.** Subscribe to consumer protection updates or follow trusted cybersecurity sources. Awareness is your best armor.
- **Consider enrolling in an identity theft protection service.** Companies like LifeLock, IdentityForce, or Aura monitor your personal information, alert you to suspicious activity, and often assist with recovery if your identity is stolen. For some, the peace of mind is worth every penny.
- **File a complaint with the Consumer Financial Protection Bureau** if you have any problems with banks, lenders, and large non-bank entities, such as credit reporting agencies and debt collection companies.

No one is immune. Whether you're booking a flight, swiping on a dating app, running a business, or simply charging your phone in an airport, scams can find you. Kim and Kathy's scam chapters shares the raw reality of how one seemingly harmless moment—plugging into a public USB port—spiraled into a full-scale identity hijacking that stole more than data. It stole time, trust, and a sense of safety. Romance scams, phishing emails, online cons—they don't care how smart, successful, or secure you are. If you're human, you're a target. That's why scam awareness isn't optional—it's a non-negotiable life skill for anyone who wants to live wisely and stay protected in today's world.

Take Care of Your Body!

Where else are you going to live?

PART 3
TAKE CARE OF YOU!

KATHY DEMPSEY

Take Care of Yourself – Physically

*If I knew I was going to live this long,
I'd have taken better care of myself.*
—Mickey Mantle

Because *your body is the only place you have to live.* Let's not sugarcoat it: your body is your home. Not your house, not your zip code—**your body**. And as our wise friend Lenny likes to say: *"Take care of your body. Where else are you going to live?"*

We've all known people who've been evicted from their bodies too soon—folks who didn't treat their physical selves with the care and respect they deserved. Let's not follow in those footsteps.

MOVE: Your Body Loves It
Movement is magic. It keeps your body alive and your mind sharp. The key isn't to run a marathon (unless you want to) it's to find something you enjoy and do it regularly. Dance in your kitchen. Walk the dog. Take a yoga class. Chase your kids around. Ride a bike. Garden. Just move.

A great sign you've built a good habit? It feels harder to skip it than to do it. That's when you know it's become part of you. And exercise doesn't just tone your muscles—it boosts your brainpower, lifts your mood, and builds your self-esteem. It's like a daily dose of self-respect.

SLEEP: Your Secret Superpower
Let's be honest—sleep is often the first thing we sacrifice, even though it should be sacred. Without enough sleep, our brains get fuzzy, our immune systems weaken, and let's face it, we get a little cranky (ok, a lot). And sleep-deprived drivers? They're as dangerous as drunk ones. Yep, a 2001 study proved it: drowsy drivers made just as many mistakes as those legally intoxicated.

So how much sleep do you actually need? Most people do well on 7–8 hours, though there's some wiggle room. The important part is making it a priority. Too often we rob ourselves of sleep and try to make up for it with caffeine and energy drinks. Spoiler: they don't work. In fact, they can mess with your natural sleep cycle and rob you of the deep, restorative sleep you really need.

Want to sleep better? Try this:
- Go to bed and wake up at the same time every day—yes, even weekends.
- Make your room cool, dark, and quiet.
- Power down your screens an hour before bed.
- Create a wind-down ritual: read, meditate, journal—whatever calms your mind.
- Skip the caffeine and alcohol near bedtime.
- Soothing music? Aromatherapy? A warm bath? Yes, yes, and yes.
- Get regular exercise—but not too late in the evening.

 **LENNY'S WISDOM:**
Think of sleep as your body's overnight repair shop. Don't skip the tune-up.

EAT WELL: Fuel, Not Filler

Healthy eating isn't about following the latest diet trend—it's about giving your body what it *really* needs. Yes, there are a million diets out there (Keto! Paleo! Mediterranean! Vegan! Breatharian?!). But let's keep it simple: **eat real food**. The fresher, the better.

At the grocery store, hang out on the outer edges—that's where the fresh fruits, veggies, and lean proteins live. The middle aisles? That's where processed foods lurk, often stuffed with sodium, sugar, and unpronounceable preservatives.

Here's a good rule of thumb:

Buy food that spoils. Eat it before it does.

Seriously, what has more life in it: a crisp apple or a cracker that's been hanging out in your cabinet since Sam Walton stocked his first Walmart! Exactly. Stanford physician Dr. Walter Bortz once advised us to "eat like a bushman." Translation? Stick to food that's as close to its natural state as possible. Fresh. Whole. Alive.

We've all heard "you are what you eat." So, ask yourself: *Do I want to be vibrant and energized—or shelf-stable and sluggish*? That doesn't mean you can't treat yourself now and then. Enjoy the burger. Savor the ice cream. Just don't let those foods take center stage. Make indulgence the exception, not the habit.

The Original Energy Drink: Water
No sugar, no crash—just pure, clean fuel your body actually wants. Water is the foundation of everything your body needs, drink up and thrive.

Every cell in your body is begging for water, don't make them beg louder. Hydration supports mood, movement, and motivation. It's not just water—it's wellness in a glass.

Most people need about half their body weight in ounces of water each day. So, if you weigh 160 pounds, aim for 80 ounces. Proper hydration helps with focus, digestion, energy levels, and even skin health. It cushions your joints, flushes toxins, and helps your body function at its best.

Feeling tired, foggy, or cranky? Sometimes, all you really need is a glass of water. Sip intentionally, your body will thank you.

Final Thought
Taking care of your physical body isn't about perfection. It's about intention. It's about making small, sustainable choices every day that add up to a big difference over time. So, move your body. Get your sleep. Eat real food.

Take Care of Yourself – Mentally

Your mind needs care just as much as your body does. One of the most powerful things you can do for your mental well-being is to learn how to live in the *present moment*. Practicing mindfulness helps quiet the mental noise and keeps you from getting stuck in the past or overwhelmed by the future.

Yoga is a great tool that supports both mind and body. It combines movement, breath, and awareness in a way that brings you back to *now*. Meditation is another powerful practice—it helps train your brain to focus, stay grounded, and respond rather than react.

Mental self-care also means keeping your thoughts in check. That inner critic? It needs a fact-checker. Start noticing irrational beliefs or negative thought patterns and replace them with positive, truthful, and hopeful alternatives. A healthy mind expects good things—not because it's naive, but because it's resilient.

Another important aspect of mental self-care is keeping your brain active and engaged. As Bob Dylan said, "As soon as you stop learning, you start dying." Keep your mind sharp and your curiosity alive. Read a new book, try crossword puzzles, take up chess, start learning a new language, or even sign up for that cooking class you've been putting off.

Other ideas?
Listen to inspiring podcasts. (Like You're Not Dead Yet – It's fabulous! Come on!) Journal your thoughts. Spend time with people who make you laugh and think. Create something—paint, write, build, or dream out loud.

Because mental self-care isn't just about surviving—it's about staying mentally agile, emotionally strong, and joyfully present.

 **LENNY'S WISDOM:**
If your brain has 42 tabs open and 3 are frozen—close some. You're not tech support for the universe.

Take Care of Yourself - Spiritually

Taking care of yourself isn't just about the body or the mind, it's about nurturing your spirit too. Tending to your spiritual well-being strengthens your inner foundation, and that's what holds you steady when life throws curveballs—or when SHED HAPPENS.

Spiritual care looks different for everyone. For some, it means prayer, meditation, or simply spending quiet time in reflection. For others, it's found in nature walks, sunrises, or moments of awe that connect them to something greater than themselves.

You might find spiritual nourishment through your faith tradition, attending services, or engaging in spiritual discussions with others who share your beliefs. Or you might cultivate it through music, art, journaling, or simply creating space in your day for stillness and gratitude.

What matters most is finding what fills your soul and making time for it regularly. Because when your spirit is grounded, you're more present, more peaceful, and more prepared to be a light for others when they need it most.

Other ways to support your spiritual self?
- Keep a gratitude journal
- Read books that inspire and challenge your worldview
- Volunteer for something that moves your heart
- Practice forgiveness—toward yourself and others
- Spend time in silence, without distractions

As the saying goes, "You can't pour from an empty cup." So, fill yours first. A strong spiritual life doesn't remove life's challenges—but it gives you the strength to face them with grace, clarity, and compassion.

 **LENNY'S WISDOM:**
If you're expecting spiritual enlightenment by next Tuesday, you might want to SHED your timeline.

Take Charge of Yourself - Financially

We've all heard the saying, "Save for a rainy day." And let's be real—rainy days **will** come, even in the driest of places like where I live in Arizona. One of life's biggest stressors, aside from when SHED HAPPENS, is being caught financially unprepared for the storms ahead.

Financial experts now recommend having at least eight months' worth of living expenses saved for emergencies. That might sound daunting, but trust me—it's worth it.

I learned this lesson the hard way. At 27, after a painful divorce, I found myself financially devastated—so much so that I had to move back in with my parents. I juggled three jobs just to dig myself out. But through sheer determination, I did. That experience taught me a lifelong habit: I committed to saving 25% of my income, 10% for short-term needs and 15% for retirement.

The first few years were tough, no doubt. But now? Living below my means is second nature—way, way below my means. And let me tell you, there's no greater peace of mind than knowing you have the financial freedom to make choices when life throws you a curveball.

And life did throw me some big ones. When COVID hit, my entire speaking business shut down overnight. Then the second blow of identity theft, which drained my accounts, locked me out of my business accounts and wiping out 27 years of building and left me fighting to reclaim my life. As if that weren't enough, health challenges followed, burying me with huge medical bills. It almost destroyed me, testing my resilience in ways I never imagined. I never expected it to take nearly five years to recover and rebuild. But do you know what saved me? Emergency savings. Without it, I wouldn't have survived.

The bottom line? Take care of yourself financially, so you have the power to take care of everything else. Because when SHED HAPPENS, you'll be ready.

LENNY'S WISDOM:
Retirement planning isn't about gold-plated bathtubs—it's about peace of mind and not Googling "Can I outlive my savings?"

Part 3: Take Care of You!

10 Financial Self-Care Tips

1. **Build an Emergency Fund** – Aim for at least eight months' worth of essential expenses. Start small if you have to, but start.
2. **Live Below Your Means** – If you're spending everything you earn, you're one crisis away from disaster.
3. **Automate Your Savings** – Set up automatic transfers to savings before you even see your paycheck.
4. **Make "Fake" Car Payments to Yourself** – Even if you don't have a car loan, pretend you do. Set aside a monthly "car payment" into a high-yield savings account. When the time comes to buy a new car, you'll have cash in hand—no interest, no debt, and no stress.
5. **Be Smart About Debt** – Debt can be a trap, especially high-interest credit cards and loans. Prioritize paying off high-interest debt first, then avoid new debt by only buying what you can afford in cash.
6. **Saving is Just the Start**—invest wisely in stocks, real estate, and retirement accounts to build lasting financial security. Diversify your income by adding a part-time job, consulting, or passive income streams.
7. **Plan for the Unexpected** – Health issues, job loss, or economic downturns will happen. It's just not if, but when—have a plan in place.
8. **Protect Your Identity** – Fraud and theft can wipe you out. Stay vigilant with strong security measures.
9. **Educate Yourself Financially** – The more you know about money, the better choices you'll make. Read, learn, and grow.
10. **Make Peace with Money** – Financial stress is real. Prioritize mental and emotional well-being by creating a plan that works for you.

If you don't organize your affairs, your family will - and it won't be pretty.

PART 4:
DYING WELL -
A GRACEFUL EXIT THAT PREVENTS CHAOS, ENDS CONFLICT, AND SECURES YOUR LEGACY

KIM HARMS

Dying Well:
The Final Act of Living Well

> *The healthiest response to death is to love,*
> *honor and celebrate life.*
> –Ira Byock

No matter what you believe happens to you after you die, you can be sure of one thing: you will die. So far there is no escape. I, for one, believe my spirit will be in a better place so I am not worried about me. However, I will leave behind people I love, and I want to show my love for them by not leaving a mess. I want them to be resilient, I want them to be happy, I want them to flourish. We don't know when our time is up, so it is important for us to be prepared. And the time to get prepared is right now!

First of all, it's time to SHED our fear of death. If you need a refresher, check out Kathy's Overcoming Fear chapter.

Some of us fear death itself and some of us fear the unknown, the pain, the loss of control, or the heartache we'll leave behind. We push it to the back of our minds, pretending we've got endless time. But avoiding the conversation doesn't make death disappear—it just makes us unprepared when it comes. Facing our mortality is about loosening fear's grip so we can live and die with greater peace. We need to acknowledge death as a part of life. It's not the enemy, but our eventual companion.

So, what can we do to minimize the fear of death and dying? According to the book, *Overcoming the Fear of Death: Through Each of the Four Main Belief Systems* by Kelvin H. Chin, the four main belief systems about death are:

Part 4: Dying Well

1. No belief in an afterlife
2. Afraid of heaven or hell
3. Looking forward to heaven
4. Belief in past lives

No matter what your belief is, making the best legacy possible while you are here and preparing your loved ones for life after you are gone is still a good idea.

Maybe we should all consider death simply a graduation from life. I have been blessed by a family that knows how to die well. My husband Jim smiled through his last days; his mother waited to pass away until she was able to say goodbye to her last two children. My sister-in-law Sylvia tried everything to stay alive but, when she was finally told that she was dying, accepted it with grace and then began to sing with her frail soprano voice The Lord Will Take Care of Me. My beautiful niece Julie, wracked with pain from an unforgiving cancer lay in her bed laughing and telling stories while we gathered for Easter dinner at the table placed at the foot of her bed.

I know from experience that by dying in a state of peace and acceptance you help make the grieving easier. On August 7, 2020 (what would have been our son Eric's 31st birthday) I was helping my husband Jim get out of our walk-in tub. He had recently been placed on hospice but we were all expecting he would last at least 6 months. He was weak and on oxygen and couldn't walk—okay maybe we just *hoped* he would make it for 6 more months.

That morning, I took his oxygen off for a couple of seconds to help get his shirt on and suddenly he slumped over in the tub. He was not breathing and did not have a pulse. I panicked and, even though he was DNR, I tried rescue breathing for about 5 minutes but to no avail. I called the hospice nurse in tears. She said she would come over to help. I then made the call to my daughter Hillary to tell her the news. We cried on the phone together for at least 10 minutes.

As we talked, I began to blame myself for Jim's death. I felt that I had failed at one of the most important jobs of my life, taking care of Jim at the end of his. If only I had not taken his oxygen off, perhaps he would still be alive. The weight of grief was heavy enough, but shame and guilt made it suffocating.

Then, all of a sudden, and 20 minutes after Jim's last breath, he took a big deep breath, just like in the movies. I shouted, "He's alive!" and dropped the phone. Jim was now breathing normally but unconscious. At the same time, the hospice nurse arrived at my home. She started saying, "I am so sorry for your loss." But I interrupted with "He's Alive!".

She burst into action and called the rescuers (thank you first responders). They got Jim into bed. After a while Jim woke up and talked to us as if nothing had happened. His body no longer worked, and he was now bed ridden but his mind was intact. I called our family and told them we were having a party, and they better get to it as we did not know how long Jim had left. They came in droves and pampered Jim with pillows, ice cream and Diet Coke; anything he wanted. Jim smiled all day even though he knew he was dying and probably soon. He passed away peacefully early the next morning.

My reaction to this second passing was different than the first Although the grief was the same, I missed him terribly, the shame and guilt were gone. I accepted the fact that his time had come and that I was not responsible, in any way, for his death. There was a certain peace in that and I was grateful for that last remaining day with Jim.

I have also witnessed death when the dying were angry they were dying. I completely understand that. It is not uncommon for people to fight until the end. That is also understandable. Every death is unique.

I would just like to ask that we consider the impact our death has on those who live on and not let our anger be misdirected at them.

The idea of a "happy death" might sound like a contradiction, but for many faith traditions, it's not only possible, it's a spiritual goal. Early Methodists believed that a well-lived life led to a well-faced death. To them, dying wasn't about fear or fanfare—it was about faith. A "happy death" meant leaving this world with peace in your soul, hymns on your lips, and loved ones by your side. In fact, Methodists often recorded the final words of the faithful to encourage others: proof that grace doesn't quit, even at the last breath.

And it's not just Methodists who hold space for a holy goodbye. The Catholics have the Last Rites, where the dying are anointed to prepare them for their transition to the afterlife. Buddhists strive to meet death with a quiet mind, often surrounded by chanting and stillness to ease the transition into the next life. Hindus recite sacred texts and chant God's name, guiding the soul toward moksha—freedom from the cycle of rebirth. In Islam, the dying are encouraged to speak the Shahada, affirming their faith as family members gently pray them into eternity. Jewish tradition invites reflection and reconciliation through the Vidui, a final prayer of confession and peace. No matter the faith, the common thread is this: a good death doesn't mean everything went according to plan. It means the heart was ready, the spirit was at peace, and love—human and divine—was present.

In a way, the modern hospice movement is our culture's long-overdue embrace of the "happy death." As mentioned earlier in this book almost 31% of Americans died at home in 2017, making it the most common site of death for the first time in decades. The use of hospice is growing.

When a cure is no longer possible, hospice steps in to offer comfort, dignity, and connection in life's final chapter. The heart of hospice care is about improving quality of life, not prolonging it at any cost. It centers on palliative care with a focus on easing pain, managing symptoms, and offering emotional and spiritual support to both the individual and their loved ones.

While many people hope to die at home, there are certain advantages to dying in a hospital setting. Hospitals offer immediate access to medical staff and advanced technology, which can provide quick relief from pain and sudden symptoms. For families who feel overwhelmed by caregiving, the hospital can offer a sense of safety, support, and structure during a difficult time. In some cases, dying in a hospital can also give loved ones more time to gather, say goodbye, and receive compassionate guidance from palliative or hospice teams trained to ease the end-of-life journey.

One of the best gifts you can give your loved ones is making sure the decision about where you want to die remains in your hands—not in the middle of a family argument. A clearly written health care directive can spare them the burden of guessing your wishes and help prevent painful conflict during an already emotional time.

Another important component of dying well is your ability to face your death, when it finally comes, with acceptance and grace, and to prepare your family to thrive after you are gone. The next chapter and the bonus workbook will help you with that!

What's Your Legacy: Building Emotional Wealth for Your Loved Ones

*Carve your name on hearts, not tombstones.
A legacy is etched into the minds of others and the stories they share about you.*
— Shannon Alder

We all understand the importance of financial life insurance—a safety net ensuring that our loved ones are financially secure when we are no longer here. But how often do we consider the emotional security of those we leave behind? They will grieve after we go, grief is an unavoidable part of loss, but there are steps we can take today to help ease the emotional burden on our loved ones after we pass.

One of the most powerful gifts we can leave behind is the assurance of love and connection. Too often, life gets in the way. Families become scattered across the country, or even across the world. We get busy, and that busyness often prevents us from expressing our affection as often as we'd like.

Harvard University completed an 80-year study of over 700 individuals and found conclusively that the most important predictors of happiness are strong social connections and close relationships. The world I grew up in, without the presence of the internet and social media, required that we relied on in-person contact for learning and also working. We had built in social structures that required our physical presence in schools, places of worship and at work which made forming strong social connections a bit easier.

The families were larger too, my husband Jim and his 13 brothers and sisters maintained close personal relationships throughout their lives. Those families had children and then grandchildren and the cycle continued. Today, the birthrate is down, and personal interaction is not required at school and at work. More and more of my peers do not have children or grandchildren. We need to work harder to develop connections.

Building Strong Relationships Now

The best emotional insurance you can provide is to build those strong relationships in the present. No amount of money can replace the comfort of knowing we were deeply loved. When my grandchildren received their first cell phones, I made a conscious effort to text them almost daily with an "I love you" theme. Sometimes, I'd send a childhood photo, a silly joke, or simply a cluster of heart emojis. The goal was simple: to let them know I love them and think of them every day. It is my hope that this small but meaningful act will leave them with an enduring sense of how much I loved them long after I am gone.

Ask yourself: What can you do today to strengthen your relationships? Have you told your family members or friends how much they mean to you? Have you taken the time to share your wisdom, your stories, and your love in ways that will last beyond your lifetime?

One way to prepare for the future and ensure your loved ones feel your presence even in your absence, consider talking about grief before it happens, and send reminders of your love that will remain even after you are gone. Here are 7 steps to help you prepare your loved ones for life without you.

1. Talking About Grief.

When talking about grief it is important to let your family know that although grief will happen, with work it will lessen over time. It is also important that you let them know that your most important legacy is for them to thrive after you are gone.

2. Writing Legacy Love Letters
Handwritten letters are a timeless way to communicate love, encouragement, and wisdom. Take the time to write letters to your children, grandchildren, and other cherished individuals. These letters can be updated over time and should reflect your hopes, prayers, and personal sentiments. I put mine in my legacy binder, carefully placed in page protectors, to be opened after my death.

3. Seeking Reconciliation and Offering Apologies
Unresolved conflicts can make grief even more difficult. Apologize while you still can, forgive now, reconcile before it is too late.

4. Preserving Family and Medical Histories
Family stories are a priceless inheritance. Document your family history, and traditions, so they can be passed down through generations. Additionally, a record of your medical history can be invaluable for your family members as they navigate their own health journeys.

5. Sharing Recipes and Keepsakes
My family loved my Macaroni and Cheese recipe; I even wrote a dental school graduation commencement address titled "Hotdish for Success" (hotdish is the Minnesota term for casserole) focused on the value of giving beyond the expected. Both daughters have adapted it to their families and hopefully it will be passed on to the next generation and even served at my funeral with the recipe attached. Compile a book of your favorite recipes and the stories behind them.

6. Preserving Memories Through Video and Books
Modern technology makes it easier than ever to create and preserve memories. My daughter compiled one for my husband and we have several books written for Eric by his friends at Columbia and his family. They are valued family treasures.
- **"This Is My Life" Video:** Record a video sharing your life story, values, and lessons learned.
- **Favorite Memories** Video: Create individual videos sharing specific memories with each loved one.

- **Goodbye Video:** Offer a heartfelt farewell message for your family.
- **Photo Book:** Compile a book of pictures with captions that narrate your life story and important family moments.

7. Preparing Special Cards and Gifts for Future Occasions

You can continue to be present in your loved ones' lives by preparing:
- **Birthday, holiday, and Valentine's Day cards** to be delivered after your passing.
- **A wrapped Christmas or birthday gift** for the first year without you.
- **Letters for milestone events** such as graduations, weddings, and the birth of a child.

Receiving a letter or gift from you during these pivotal moments will reinforce your enduring love and presence. For events such as a marriage or having children which may or may not happen, put these letters in the possession of a trusted friend to be given out only if the event occurs.

The Power of Preparation and Love

We can't control when we will leave this world, but we can control how we prepare for it. Building emotional wealth is designed to soften the impact of loss through love, preparation, and intentionality, to equip our loved ones with the tools they need to move forward and flourish after we are gone.

So, ask yourself today: What can you do to strengthen your relationships and leave an emotional legacy that lasts a lifetime?

Remember, death comes unexpectedly, none of us are getting out of here alive. Might as well be ready. Don't let your last words be, "Wait, I meant to write that down…"

Part 4: Dying Well

(**Spoiler alert:** There is a lot more to dying well. Everything you need to know and do is listed in the bonus workbook. Complete it for your family and die like a legend!)

For additional resources and downloads, visit:
www.YoureNotDeadYet.Life/LegacyWorksheets

Closing Thoughts: Your Invitation to Begin Now

By Kim Harms & Kathy Dempsey

We've shared our stories, our tears, our tools, and our truths. Now, it's your turn.

This book—and the podcast that complements it—is not meant to sit quietly on a shelf. It's meant to stir something in you. A spark. A question. A courageous step forward. It's a call to action, and the time to respond is now.

Don't wait for tragedy to clarify what matters. Don't let another week pass before having that conversation, writing that letter, booking that trip, forgiving that wound, or shedding what no longer serves you. Whether you're 35 or 85, whether you're thriving or struggling—**this moment is your starting line**.

We challenge you:
- Take one idea from this book and put it into practice this week.
- Start a "Living Well" conversation with someone you love.
- Reflect on what it would mean for you to graduate life with honors.
- Listen to an episode of the *You're Not Yet Dead* podcast and let it stretch you.
- Complete the BONUS: You're Not Dead Yet! WORKBOOK that follows.

Because here's the truth: **YoureNotDeadYet.Life is more than a movement—it's a wake-up call to live fully, laugh often, and graduate life with honors.**

You don't have to have all the answers. You just have to begin.

Part 4: Dying Well

So go ahead—take that step. Live your life on purpose, with grace, with joy, and with your eyes wide open.

We're cheering you on every step of the way.

With love and gratitude,

Kim Harms & Kathy Dempsey

My cousin Benny went extinct last year. Great guy! Never saw it coming. Wasn't prepared. Don't be like Benny.

The End!

You're Not Dead Yet!

Congratulations!

You've finished the book. Now it's time to finish your legacy plan so your family doesn't finish each other!

Lenny Jr.

You're Not Dead Yet! Workbook

ONE BINDER TO RULE THEM ALL!

Downloadable pages available at
www.YoureNotDeadYet.Life/LegacyWorksheets

My Action Plan

What: _____

By When: _____

Action Step:_____

Support/Accountability Person: _____

To download the worksheets, visit:
www.YoureNotDeadYet.Life/LegacyWorksheets

Workbook

KIM HARMS

An Important Workbook to Spare Your Family Pain and Provide Them Peace

You can download these pages at
YoureNotDeadYet.Life/LegacyWorksheets and
add them to your legal binder for easy reference.

Imagine your family after your passing. They're lost, mourning, and overwhelmed. They may have even argued over whether you died in a hospital or in hospice. Then, as they search through your belongings for your will, passwords, the title to your car—critical documents needed to manage your estate—they can't find them, or worse, they realize that no will exists at all. What follows is a descent into a legal and financial maze, a nightmare that fuels confusion, distress, and conflict.

How many families have had their grief compounded by chaos and bitterness and anger at each other simply because a parent or loved one failed to prepare? We have the power to prevent this. It is our responsibility to "clean up our mess" and get ready for the future.

How do we do that? There are just 4 important steps, and they should all be started immediately.

The 1st step is to get your affairs in order. Make sure you have a healthcare directive in place, your will is written and updated regularly. Gather important documents like financial accounts, passwords, and contact lists, and keep them in one place. (We recommend a legacy binder)

Step two is to define your legacy. Hopefully you will be leaving important values like resilience, laughter, hard work, or kindness, but the greatest legacy you can leave is love. Tell your children you love them. Tell them often.

The third step is to talk. Preparing your family for life without you requires having difficult conversations about both death and grief. Yes, it's uncomfortable, but it's absolutely necessary.

And finally step 4, straighten out any emotional baggage you do not want to leave behind. Apologize while you still can. Forgive before it's too late. Reconcile now. Capture your family history, wisdom, your love, in legacy videos, books, or letters.

Assembling a legacy workbook is an act of love for your family. Everyone has their own system, but for me a large three ring binder with every page enclosed in a plastic page protector works best. The page protectors serve not only to safeguard the documents but to hold small important papers, like your social security card, the titles to your car or even the Valentines you prepare to remind your loved ones how grateful you were for their presence in your life. This last bonus section of the book gives you everything you need to assemble your legacy binder. To make it even simpler we are including a free downloadable, easy to fill out Death Preppers Checklist on our website. These pages are ready for download at YoureNotDeadYet.life/LegacyWorksheets—add them to your binder and take one more step toward peace of mind.

Besides the recommendations outlined in the workbook, it is also essential to include all the documents that your family will need to manage your estate like insurance policies, real estate documents, titles, marriage records, identity cards (or copies of them), birth certificates...the list goes on. The page protectors help keep these documents safe. Anything that you think your family will need either to settle your physical estate or emotional estate needs to be included in this binder. The surprising part to me was how little time it took to fill out the forms and organize the documents.

Ideally the next step is to make backup copies of these documents (physically or electronically) and let those responsible for managing your estate know where they are located. I have my documents located in a fireproof safe and both of my daughters have the combination.

When I die, I hope my children and grandchildren feel the depth of my love in every detail I've prepared to make their lives easier. But just in case the files and forms don't say it loud enough, they'll find letters and little Valentines tucked away, my final way of whispering, "I love you" one more time. What messages will you send to your family?

This workbook is designed to help you build your legacy, improve your relationships, get your affairs in order and talk to your family about death.

The life expectancy of the average human is over 40 million minutes. Each one of those minutes represents a memory, an impression, a legacy. But eventually, our minutes run out, and the story of our lives continues only in the hearts and minds of those left behind. How many minutes do you have left? Death comes unexpectedly. Don't assume you have time. By preparing today, you give your family a most valuable blessing—a clear path forward, free from confusion and conflict. This isn't just a task—it's a beautiful gift that will last long after you're gone.

The clock keeps ticking.
The time to get ready is now!

KIM HARMS
Death Prepper's Goal-Setting Guide

The dread of doing a task uses up more time and energy than doing the task itself.
—Rita Emmet

Directions: Cross off tasks you do not want to do. Check off tasks already accomplished. Work with your group (or individually) to develop a plan to finish all the tasks you wish to do. Three asterisks will follow subjects where detailed information is provided later on. Death Prepper's Checklist:

___ have a discussion with your family regarding your wishes
___ name of executor
___ name of accountant
___ name of attorney
___ name of tax preparer
___ name of a financial advisor
___ name of health care provider
___ prepare a power of attorney
___ Living Will/Health Care Directive***
___ Last Will and Testament***
___ personal information (Legal name, maiden name, social security number, birthplace, spouse's name, former spouse's name, children's names)
___ location of will, passport, driver's license, birth certificate, keys, marriage certificate (Ideally, have copies of all important documents in your legacy folder/binder)
___ location of valuables
___ safe and combination or location of keys
___ historical information (parents' names and birthplaces)
___ insurance for burial expenses, if applicable
___ employee benefits

Workbook

___ make sure appropriate beneficiaries are listed for bank accounts, retirement accounts, life insurance, etc., to ensure access to your funds
___ organ/tissue donation***
___ list of investments
___ real estate owned or leased and details
___ cars (VIN number, title/ lease location, key location, make, year, and model)
___ boats and other vehicles and identifying information, location of keys
___ firearms (location and description)
___ list of passwords
___ list of bank accounts
___ list of credit cards numbers, account numbers, online usernames, and passwords
___ list of email and social media usernames and passwords
___ list of life insurance policies
___ list utilities (gas, electric, water, phone)
___ health insurance information (keep a copy of your card in your folder)
___ access to documents plan
___ share legacy information***
___ decide upon living wake, funeral, both? ***
___ religious affiliation, home church
___ choose and arrange burial***
___ traditional
___ cremation
___ natural
___ burial at sea
___ aquamation
___ composting
___ sky burial
___ become a diamond, cryonics, etc.
___ space burial
___ secure burial plot

Consider pre-arranging your funeral to make things easier for your heirs

___ military service, if applicable
___ if a veteran, secure the appropriate papers for burial benefits
___ select pallbearers
___ write an obituary (or give information to someone else to write) ***
___ select your obituary picture***
___ if a business owner, ensure your business is ready for the transition
___ if a business owner, business name, location, bank, accountant, attorney, contracts, employees' names and contact information, lease, keys, usernames and pass-words, business credit cards, financial records, accounts receivables, income stream
___ if a business owner/partner, make sure your heirs understand transition plans
___ list of people to notify and social media announcement (Perhaps develop a calling system)
___ make your own meme-morial (A meme is basically a short video or image or piece of writing that is usually humorous and spreads rapidly on the internet.)
___ list of creditors: itemize personal loans, names, detailed information
___ notify parties included in your will
___ give directions or fill out the forms necessary for securing the property you own such as stopping the mail
___ put you on the deceased, do not contact list
___ cancel services etc., driver's license, SSN, passport
___ important bills that need to be paid
___ closing digital accounts
___ compile a list of assets
___ list the location of important items
___ address the payment of income and real estate taxes
___ develop a system to distribute assets not covered by your will
___ pet names, license info, veterinarian
___ list pet names, license information, veterinarian

Workbook

___ work out pet care for when you are gone. Give special instructions
___ set aside payment for someone to "clean up" what remains (Refer to "The Legacy of Shedding" chapter)
___ specify location and information about storage units
___ if you have a monument, decide what you want to put on it***
___ Other_____
___ Other_____
___ Other_____

To download the worksheets, visit:
www.YoureNotDeadYet.Life/LegacyWorksheets

You're Not Dead Yet!

KIM HARMS

The Grateful but Not Yet Dead Tour:
Why Wait for the Funeral to Tell People You Love them?

Make sure you tell the people you love that you love them. Loudly and often. You never know when it might be too late.
—Tom Hiddleston

My dear friend and partner in legacy building, Terri Hands, came up with a unique way to show her gratitude. She gathered old photos of her high school days and brought them with her to her high school class reunion. Imagine the gaiety and happiness those pictures brought to the recipients. Do you have a special place to visit and special people to express your gratitude to?

After I lost my ability to practice dentistry, I planned two grateful but not yet dead tours. My first was to my mother's hometown, Cincinnati, Ohio, to visit her only living brother, my Uncle Tom, and his family. Tom was the last living uncle, and he played a big role in my life when we lived with my mother. He was now extremely ill and in hospice at home. His hospital bed was placed prominently in the living room, a clear indication that he did not want to miss anything going on in his home. His wife, my still red-headed Aunt Ruth, although frail herself, took loving care of him. If he needed to be lifted or bathed, his sons showed up.

When I told my uncle who I was (it had been about forty years since he had last seen me), he started to cry. I was able to tell Tom how grateful I was for the time and attention he paid to me as a child and his inclusion of my brother, sister and me in his family activities. I described specific events, including learning to swim in his swimming pool and crashing my bike at the bottom of the hill in front of his house. I was also able to thank Aunt Ruth for her wonderful cooking and fun-loving personality.

My second trip was to my last living uncle on my father's side of the family. Uncle Jack and Aunt Hazel were wonderful. They told me tales of my father, and their love for my mother and gave me pictures and mementos of my grandparents. During these sojourns, I had life-affirming discussions, collected new stories and new photographs of my early life, and brought love and comfort to my aging uncles and aunts.

My friend from fourth grade, Nancy, called me recently and planned a grade school reunion in her new hometown of Lewis, Delaware. It was fabulous! Even after fifty years and a wide range of career choices, we all reverted to our fourth-grade selves and had a wonderful time together. We then planned our next one in the Northwoods of Minnesota. It was fabulous! There's something magical—borderline miraculous—about gathering with the people who knew you in 4th grade, especially when they still remember your unfortunate bowl cut and love you anyway. It's like time travel with more wrinkles.

Are there aging aunts or uncles or others in your life you would like to thank? Do you have younger friends or relatives who need to know how much you love them? Are you anxious to reconnect with a special group of friends from your past? Consider planning your own Grateful but Not Yet Dead Tour.

Planning Your Grateful But Not Yet Dead Tour: A Practical Checklist

1. Identify Your People
Decide which group or groups you'd like to reconnect with—friends, family members, former classmates, or colleagues. Make a list of the individuals you'd like to include.

2. Choose a Convenient Location
Select a location that's accessible and comfortable for the group. Consider travel time, mobility needs, and availability.

3. Determine the Right Setting
Would your gathering work best in a hotel, a vacation rental, someone's home, or a familiar family spot? Think about group size and privacy needs.

4. Find a Point Person
Is there someone in the group who enjoys organizing events or would be willing to help coordinate details?

5. Gather Photos and Mementos
Bring along meaningful items like photos, letters, keepsakes, or memorabilia that can spark conversation and shared memories.

6. Prepare a Gratitude Message
Consider writing a short letter or list of the specific reasons you are grateful for this group. Sharing it during the gathering can be meaningful.

7. Share a Legacy
Think about what you might want to leave behind—words of wisdom, stories, small gifts, or anything that reflects the impact these people have had on your life.

8. Do it now!

KIM HARMS
The Exit Interview You Need To Plan Now

Thinking and talking about death need not be morbid; they may be quite the opposite. Ignorance and fear of death overshadow life, while knowing and accepting death erases this shadow.
— Lily Pincus

Talking about our death is hard. But not talking about what is inevitable while we are still here (and our brains are still functioning) may result in unnecessary pain, suffering, conflict, and chaos for those who live on. Let's face it; we do not like to talk about life and death decisions, and certainly not when it is *our* life and death we are talking about. Be prepared for different reactions from different family members.

Your family needs to know where your death-prepping information is; they need to know the philosophy behind your decisions, and they need to know how and where you want to spend your last days.

One advantage of this discussion is that you will learn how your family responds to your wishes. If you spend the time and effort to have a comprehensive death planning folder in place, what good will it do if no one knows where to access it? Also, what if your loved ones object to how you wish to spend your last days? Having this discussion will allow you to reinforce your wishes and/or make any changes you feel are necessary.

The debate over seeking every measure possible to sustain life or taking the hospice route may become emotional, but better to have it while you can participate (as the ultimate decision maker) rather than when you are no longer able to make or express such decisions.

One of the best books I have read on the subject of aging was the bestselling book, *Being Mortal: Medicine and What Matters in the End* by Atul Gawande, MD. It might be a good idea to give this book as a gift at Thanksgiving and engage in a family discussion around Christmas. Or you can use other traditional family gathering time or schedule a meeting specifically to discuss these issues. You could even suggest the meeting as a wonderful Mother's or Father's Day gift to you. There are also numerous YouTube videos, streaming movies, or this book to help educate your family.

Don't be disappointed if you meet resistance when discussing the future. All you can do is try. If someone is completely dismissive, then consider expressing your views in a letter. The important thing is to do your best!

Until now, we have been discussing your death, but what if you fear your parent or grandparent has not planned well or has not talked to you about their desires, and you would like them to express their wishes to you? Why not ask them?

This process can be relatively simple if they are open to discussion or extremely difficult if they are not. As we age, the thought of losing our independence or, worse yet, dying can be terrifying. We know in our minds that our death will happen someday, but we may not accept that it will happen to us anytime soon. Broaching the topic of your loved one's death may cause an emotional reaction that you are both unprepared for. Find a quiet time with just the two of you. Be gentle; this is a tough issue for many.

One discussion will not be enough. Be the engine that starts the conversation and strive to keep the discussions open, respectful, and informative. Only you can do this. Don't procrastinate. We think we will always have time, but at some point, for all of us, our time will run out. Will your family be meeting for a big event soon? Is there an appropriate time you can schedule a "planning for the future" meeting? By framing this as a "future planning" meeting rather than

Workbook

a "death planning" meeting, you may reduce the discomfort! Don't wait! You can do this!! I've even included a sample invitation available for download at You'reNotDeadYet.Life/LegacyWorksheets.

You're Invited!
A Heartfelt and Lighthearted Family Conversation About End-of-Life Wishes

Before I trade in my to-do list for eternal rest, let's gather for a conversation that matters. We'll laugh, maybe cry, and definitely make sure no one argues over who gets grandma's cake plate.

What We'll Cover:
- What brings me peace and how you can carry that forward
- The music, messages, and memories I'd love to leave behind
- My funeral (yes, the playlist matters!)
- Where to find the important stuff (hint: not just in the junk drawer)
- How to avoid chaos and conflict when the time comes
- This isn't about doom and gloom— it's about love, laughter, and a little logistical clarity.
- Come for the stories. Stay for the snacks. Leave with peace of mind.

DATE: [Insert Date]
TIME: [Insert Time]
LOCATION: [Insert Location]
Kindly RSVP:
- ☐ I'll be there with bells on (and maybe a notepad).
- ☐ Count me in—I'll bring tissues and snacks.
- ☐ Yes! I've always wanted to attend a "pre-funeral."
- ☐ Can't make it, but please don't leave me in charge of anything confusing.
- ☐ I'll pretend this never happened and act surprised later.

Let's talk before I'm "Toast"!

KIM HARMS

Your Last Will and Testament: Where Do Your Valuables Go?

Always plan ahead. It wasn't raining when Noah built the ark.
— Richard Cushing

I am a dentist, not an attorney; the information in this chapter is not legal advice, just observation. Please see an appropriately licensed attorney to write your Last Will and Testament and advise you on estate planning.

We are all aware of families being torn apart because parents or grandparents never quite got around to writing a Last Will and Testament. There are also many families who were so surprised at the division of property that they contested the will. In some cases, the cost of adjudicating such situations left the families penniless and the lawyers rich. If we love those we leave behind, shouldn't we ease the transition by providing a solid framework to divide our possessions?

Jim and I wanted to ensure that our deaths did not damage our daughters' beautiful relationship. We wrote our wills with a fifty-fifty split and sent them to both girls to examine before we signed them. Our mandate was: "Speak now or forever hold your peace."

After my will was signed, I sat down with my daughters, brought any jewelry I had to the table, and let each girl choose a piece in turn. The choices were written down and attached to my will so there would be no controversy after my death. I thought there would be many other possessions my girls would want and consider valuable, but the sad reality is they do not want my stuff. Like many baby boomers, I thought at least the beautiful china sets I had collected over forty-four years of marriage would be considered precious heirlooms. They are not. I have heard rumors that beautiful china is becoming appreciated again. I hope that rumor is true.

When your survivors are already established and have their own homes, it is common for them to look at the disposal of your property as a major burden.

The fact is that I raised two beautiful daughters with their own homes and their own tastes and no room for additional furniture or accessories. I can choose to celebrate their independence or bemoan the fate of my "stuff." I choose to celebrate my independent daughters.

I am leaving some "clean-up" money in my will specifically designated to cover disposal after my family has selected the valuables they want. This could then be used to pay a family member or professional company to hold an estate sale and take the pressure off my children.

Compared to many, my family was easy. My children are self-sufficient, and there are only two. They also get along well. If a family has a special needs child that may require an income, if the family is blended, or if one member of the family has worked to promote a family business, it may get complicated. There are many other complicating factors, such as kids who don't get along, no apparent heirs, or the deceased wish to donate a large sum to charity. You can do a lot to ease problems following your death by helping your heirs understand the thinking behind your decisions before your death through letter of intent. (See below, next chapter.) You don't need to share specific amounts unless you wish to, but surprises, such as uneven distribution among siblings, a large charitable donation, or unexpected inheritors, are easier to accept if they are logical in nature and explained before your death.

It is also important to consider what happens if there is a divorce and a remarriage or remarriage after one spouse dies. My husband Jim was an extrovert extraordinaire. He did not like being alone. We all knew that if I died first, Jim would want to remarry. I just asked him not to look for my replacement until after my funeral.

We considered this possibility when we wrote our wills. The most important possession that had sentimental value for us was our lake home. We built it to be a retirement home, but due to illness, disability, and our need to be near our grandchildren, our condo took over that role.

The girls wanted to make sure our cabin stayed with the family, and we agreed. In our will, the cabin was placed in a trust in my name. If I died first, Jim could live in the cabin until his death, but the ownership would belong to our daughters. In this way, the cabin would be protected from being lost to the family that built it. These are important things to consider, as well as a prenuptial or postnuptial agreement when getting remarried so that there are no surprises for the new spouse or the children.

Your attorney will draw up your will to include many things, such as your family history: are you married, are there children, how you will pay your debts, who will receive your assets and how they will receive them, guardianship of your children, and who you want as the executor to manage the distribution of the assets.

Having an easily authenticated will drafted by a knowledgeable attorney will help you avoid much of the cost of probate. The American Bar Association has some great tips. Check out their website at www.americanbar.org.

Probate is the court-supervised process that your will undergoes after you pass away. If you have a will, this process is much easier as your desires are expressed in the will. Without a will, it is much harder to determine who the executor will be or how to distribute the assets. Once again, The American Bar Association is a great resource.

If you don't yet have a will, please create one. It will cost far less in attorney's fees to draw up your will than it will cost in attorney's fees for your loved ones to try and figure (or fight) things out after you die.

KIM HARMS
Letter of Intent/Instruction

A good plan is like a road map: it shows the final destination and usually the best way to get there.
— H. Stanley Judd

According to the AARP, a letter of intent is "a flexible, informal supplement to your will that covers more personal information than what is included in your will. You don't need a lawyer to draft a letter of instruction, and you can easily change it as your circumstances or wishes change."

In the letter, it is a good idea to specify that if there is any confusion between what is said in the will or letter of intent, the will prevails. If there are any possibilities that there may be hard feelings when the contents of the will are revealed, the reasons for the disparities should be explained. This can frequently happen when the family is blended or if one member has health issues that may require special support. Sometimes one child has been given money to help with a major purchase earlier, and the parents attempt to "even things out" in the will.

If a friend or family member has taken responsibility for the care of an elderly or ill person, especially if they have not been paid for that care while it was occurring, there may be provisions made in the will to compensate that person. It would be a good idea to explain the reasoning behind this decision in a letter of intent to minimize conflict that may occur.

I have heard letters of intent used to express anger or frustration at family members. I don't recommend this. If something occurs that causes you to decide to leave someone out of your will who would expect to be included, explain your reasoning in as positive or neutral way as possible. Being matter of fact, by explaining that because of specific behavior demonstrated by a family member, you have chosen not to include them in the will is better than no explanation and also better than using a demeaning or angry tone. Keep your memory as positive as possible. Your family will thank you!

Sample Letter of Instruction

Dear [Name of Executor or Loved One],

First, thank you. I know this isn't an easy time, and I'm grateful you're willing to take on the responsibility of settling my affairs with love and care. This letter isn't a legal document, but I hope it will help make your job a little easier and your heart a little lighter.

You'll find my official will [insert location, e.g., in the brown folder in the top drawer of my desk / with my attorney, [name and contact info]. My health care directive, power of attorney, and life insurance information as well as all of the information you will need to manage my estate are located in my Legacy Binder. The Legacy Binder is in my safe. The combination is (12345).

Here are a few instructions and wishes that you may need now:

Funeral/Memorial Preferences:
I would prefer [e.g., cremation with ashes scattered at Lake Harriet]. I'd love [insert music, speakers, or rituals] at my service. Please make it a celebration of life—not just a mourning of my death.

People to Notify:
Please let [list names and contact info] know of my passing. I'd especially appreciate [Name] being told personally.

Important Contacts:
My lawyer is [name, phone/email]. My financial advisor is [name, phone/email].

Online and Digital Accounts:
A list of my passwords and accounts is stored [insert location or service]. Please close or memorialize social media accounts, and back up important family photos stored online.

Sentimental Items:
Though my will covers major items, I'd like [Name] to have [item, e.g., my grandmother's quilt]. These things hold stories, and I want them to be in the hands of those who will cherish them.

Personal Words:
To each of you reading this, please know I love you deeply. My greatest hope is that my passing doesn't cause division but brings you closer together. Forgive each other quickly. Laugh often. And live fully. I've had a beautiful life, and I leave it with peace and gratitude.

With all my love,
[Your Name]

To download the worksheets, visit:
www.YoureNotDeadYet.Life/LegacyWorksheets

KIM HARMS
Getting Rid of Your Other Stuff

*We make a living by what we get;
we make a life by what we give.*
— Winston Churchill

Ideally, you have been working on getting rid of your unused stuff before you go. (See "SHED" chapter.) But just in case you have been caught with your closets brimming, consider adding an addendum to your will and put aside money specifically allocated to dispose of your belongings not wanted by your heirs. My plan is to give my children time to take what they want from my storage areas, and then I will include money in the will to hire a professional group to sell what is valuable and dispose of the rest.

One way to distribute valuables that are not itemized in your will before the estate sale would be to label them to indicate where you wish them to go. Whatever method you choose, it is important that the family feel that the distribution is done in an equitable manner.

Sometimes there is an item that is particularly valuable and wanted by several heirs. One way to find a resolution is to establish a fair price for the item, hold a lottery to choose who can buy the item, and then add the proceeds from the sale to the estate, to be divided up according to the terms of the will. Nurse Jackie Pederson's family hosts a gathering and dice game to decide who will inherit family heirlooms. Each item is presented (like in an auction). If one person wants the item, their name is attached to it. If more than one person wants an item, they roll dice. The highest number wins. Everything gets recorded, and potential family turmoil is avoided. Get creative to find a system that works for you.

Frequently one family member, because of their geographic proximity to the deceased, finds themselves responsible for sifting through

Workbook

rooms of "stuff" for months or even years. By delegating this task and providing the funding for a professional to take care of it, you can prevent any dissension or resentment that might arise.

Removal of your unwanted belongings is a growing industry. Check out your local estate sale companies and moving services; many of them are adding disposal services and even apps!

Start now!

To download the worksheets, visit:
www.YoureNotDeadYet.Life/LegacyWorksheets

KIM HARMS
Healthcare Directives

Planning is bringing the future into the present so that you can do something about it now.
– Alan Lakein

Please do not consider this legal advice. Always consult with your state laws, and if you move, fill out a new directive that works in your new state.

Advance Healthcare Directive

Several weeks before he passed away, my husband Jim decided to enter hospice care. At that time, he worked with his nurse to develop an advance healthcare directive, which would not only ensure his wishes were followed but would also give our children and me the blessing of not having to second-guess our role in his care. When someone you love is dying, it is not unusual to want to do everything possible to keep them alive as long as possible. Hospice care focuses on the quality of life rather than the length of life. Jim's healthcare directive ensured that he died the way he wanted.

A healthcare directive allows you to express your wishes in case you cannot express those desires due to injury or illness. It also allows you to appoint a person to make these decisions if you cannot. It is helpful to discuss your wishes with your entire family, to avoid uncomfortable surprises at a stressful time if you become ill.

An advance healthcare directive is accessible online for every state on https://www.caringinfo.org/planning/advance-directives/ and can be found by searching your state name.

Each state differs in its requirements, but typically a healthcare directive requires that it be written, include your name, designate an agent to make decisions for you if you cannot, and be signed by witnesses or be notarized.

Advance directives allow you to express your views and values about healthcare in general and the types of medical treatment you would or would not want in specific circumstances. You may also include whether or not you wish to donate your organs.

An advance healthcare directive does not expire, but you should review it periodically. You should also ensure that it is easily accessible to those close to you, as it is only helpful if your healthcare providers have access to it. You can file copies with your hospital and your family, clergy, or friends. There are now digital forms of your directive that can be available on demand, including MedicAlert and even an app on your iPhone or android devices. (Once again, there's an app for that!)

Do Not Resuscitate Order: DNR

A DNR (Do Not Resuscitate) is a medical order that needs to be signed by a doctor, nurse practitioner, or physician's assistant under the direction of a physician. Laws vary by state, and it is important for you to be aware of the laws in your state and comply with them. Some states have the availability to have a DNR order printed that can be carried in your wallet.

Physician's Order For Life-Sustaining Treatment: POLST

A POLST would be appropriate if you had a serious illness and needed a DNR (Do Not Resuscitate) order or an order concerning feeding tubes or mechanical ventilation. A POLST is completed in consultation with your doctor and must be signed by your doctor. These medical orders travel with you and can be used if you need care unexpectedly outside your home area.

Most states honor a POLST, but not all. Check the POLST website to see if POLST is honored in your state. Another difference between a

POLST and an advance healthcare directive is that a POLST will be honored by an EMT. The difference between a POLST and a DNR order is that a DNR order only covers resuscitation. Typically, POLST orders are printed on bright pink paper. They should be posted on the refrigerator or otherwise readily available to the EMTs.

One of the things that I learned about a person in hospice is that the first person to call in an emergency is the hospice nurse. The nurse will contact the EMTs. There is a specific code for hospice that the nurse will give to the EMTs to alert the team that the patient they are caring for is in hospice and, in Jim's case, had a DNR order. If I had called 911 directly without a POLST or DNR order clearly evident when Jim died, the rescuers would have had to perform CPR and try to resuscitate him, even though his entire body was shutting down. The pressure required to provide compressions on a man his age and physical condition would most likely break his ribs or bruise his lungs. If he survived, he could end up on a ventilator and die in a hospital, which he did not want. By having a clear healthcare directive in place and working through the hospice system, he died peacefully the way he wanted, at home.

It is critical to note that there are no right or wrong ways to die. Many choose to have everything done to keep them alive as long as possible, and it is wonderful that we have that ability. I am glad my husband made his wishes known and documented so that I would not have to add the guilt of making a wrong decision to the grief of losing him. Thank you, Jim!

No healthcare directive? Get ready for a family feud - LIVE from your bedside!

Don't leave your loved ones guessing—write your advance healthcare directive now, so your voice is heard even when you can't speak.

KIM HARMS
Organ Donation

*Don't take your organs to heaven; heaven
knows we need them here.*
—Maxie Scully

According to the US government, 106,000 people in the United States are on the National Transplant Waiting List, and seventeen people die each day waiting. It is estimated that one donor can save up to eight lives and enhance seventy-five lives.

I first encountered the miracle of organ donation when I did a Dental General Practice Residency at Loyola University Medical Center in 1985. The heart transplant program was just starting there, and the dental residents rotated through the cardiac program. Before being added to the transplant list, every patient had to be clear of infection, including dental infection. Through the pre-immunosuppressive therapy evaluation we provided for every patient, we had the splendid honor of getting to know them. Every patient, including some children, faced a certain death without the transplant and an uncertain future with the transplant. Because transplants were not yet readily available throughout the country, there was little long-term data on survival. The patients I met faced their destinies with great courage. It was astonishing to see the transformation from fatigued, pale, and weak to robust, pink-cheeked, and healthy with the addition of a new heart.

According to the Mayo Clinic, the current survival rate after a heart transplant is about 90 percent after one year and 80 percent after five years for adults, and approximately 50 percent survive for more than thirteen years. Approximately 75 percent of people live for at least five years after liver transplants.

Those statistics became even more real for me when my husband Jim was diagnosed with liver cancer in 2007. Because a remarkable man from

Wisconsin, who was involved in a car accident, had marked "donor" on his license, Jim got a new liver. My daughters and I were able to laugh, cry, have adventures with, and be supported by our husband and father for twelve more years. Jim could see his daughters get married and meet all six of his grandchildren. He loved to point out that he had two sets of DNA, as the donated organ still retained the donor's DNA. He also speculated that if the donated organ were still in good shape when he died, it could be donated again, and theoretically live forever! His doctors told him, however, that they do not transplant an organ more than once.

Typically, solid organ donation can only occur when the patient is in a controlled environment, such as a hospital or an inpatient hospice located within a hospital, where organ recovery can occur at the time of death. Tissues, such as skin, bone, heart valves, and eyes, can be donated up to twenty-four hours following death. Sadly, when Jim died, none of his tissues were acceptable. He had used them all up.

Amy Peele, a former transplant coordinator and current award-winning murder mystery writer, explains, "The most important decision you can make is to let your family and loved ones know if you want to be an organ and tissue donor. Your family will always be asked, but it makes it a lot easier on them if you've already made that decision and communicated it to them."

I am an organ donor, and if I choose hospice for my last days and my organs are healthy enough to donate, I will request a hospice attached to a hospital. The ability to donate is important to me.

KIM HARMS

Do You Want a Party or a Living Wake?

> *A living funeral: like a roast,
> but with less fire and more Kleenex.*
> –Unknown

Remember my husband Jim who died twice? In between his two deaths, we had a party. I called all of his family to let them know that he had weakened tremendously. Those who were in town dropped what they were doing and came to visit. We contacted the rest via Zoom. It was a fabulous day and one that I will never forget. Jim was able to say good-bye to everyone either in person or virtually. This was not a planned living wake (more like an impromptu one), but it served the same purpose.

A living wake allows you to say your goodbyes. If you are in hospice or suffer from a terminal illness, would you like to see those important to you one last time? If so, perhaps you can arrange to throw one last party! It doesn't have to be complicated. You can throw together a simple potluck, go to your favorite restaurant or get carryout.

A wake is typically an informal time of remembrance and visitation, while a funeral is more formal in nature with rituals and structure.

You can also bring in officiants and have a formal living funeral. Some choose to have a eulogy, a religious ceremony, and a formal good-bye. You can even have your guests sign your coffin or write notes to include in the coffin (which you can read!). The choices are endless.

My daughter, Hillary, promised me that she will throw me a seventieth birthday party in her new house. My life expectancy is currently eighty-six, so I hope to have many years left, but celebrations for significant birthdays are important, especially as we age. For Jim's seventieth birthday in November of 2019, we had planned a trip to Turkey and Greece with our church.

Unfortunately, Jim's health would not allow an overseas adventure that required walking. Instead, we went to Universal Studios and rented a motorized cart for Jim. We had a great time. In January 2020, Hillary and I were asked to speak in Hawaii, and we took all of the adults for a fabulous week. A month after that, COVID hit, and we were grounded. By August 2020, Jim was gone. The pictures we have of Jim on his last great adventures are priceless.

Naomi Rhode tells the tale of her mother-in-law, who insisted on three parties when she turned ninety. She specified to Naomi the details she expected, including ninety attendees at the party to be held at Naomi's house. Naomi complied. I think I will do the same when I turn eighty, just in case I don't make it to ninety. You never know! Hillary, are you reading this?

Death can come suddenly, preventing the opportunity to plan a living wake. However, if this idea appeals to you, make sure you express your wishes in your legacy folder.

There is never a better time to throw a party than when you are alive!

KATHY DEMPSEY
Would You Consider a Living Funeral?

Remember Ron? You met him in the foreword. He's the one who cracked jokes while cancer cracked his body... who serenaded me with an air guitar from a hospice bed... who showed all of us how to die well by living well—right up to the last breath.

When Ron arrived at the hospice, he had one final request. Not for more medication.

Not for quiet. Not for solitude. He looked at me with his signature twinkle and said, "**I want to be at my own funeral.**"

That was Ron. Bold. Curious. Funny as ever. And honest. So, within 24 hours, we made it happen. The hospice team got Ron upright in a chair—propped up and bundled in a warm blanket. His breath was shallow, but his spirit? On fire. That day, the room filled with the sacred sounds of a life being honored *while* it was still being lived.

There were belly laughs. There were tears. There were stories we'd never heard and memories that danced between joy and grief. Ron spoke. We spoke. He said his goodbyes. We said ours.

There were hugs, inside jokes, silent prayers and music surrounded the gathering. It was interactive, intimate, and electric. He got to hear what he meant to us. He felt the love. And he *left* knowing he mattered.

Sometime later, I found myself in a very similar place. Only this time, the dying man was my dear friend and mentor, Bob Pike—a legend in the world of training and a man whose wisdom helped shape my speaking career and my life.

Bob had just entered hospice care. And I gently asked, "Would you like a Living Funeral, like Ron had?" Without hesitation, he lit up and said, "That would be awesome. It's probably the best things I'll ever hear about myself."

And oh, was it ever. His house was filled with over 100 people. Another 400 joined by Zoom from all over the world. People flew in. People dialed in. People showed up.

And what followed? A symphony of *Bob-ness*. Laughter that shook the windows. Tears that softened the edges. Stories that reminded us why this man mattered so deeply to so many.

At the end of it all, his wife turned to me, eyes glistening, and said, **"This was the BEST gift Bob ever gave me."**

Link to Bob Pike's Living Funeral:
https://youtu.be/d5LyvuTOqm8

I've now led many living funerals, each one as unique as the soul being celebrated. And believe it or not, I even have a waiting list.

Yep, people in their 40s and 50s have already told me, *"When the time comes, you're my girl."* One even joked, *"I'm not planning to die anytime soon, but I want to lock in the good lighting and a killer playlist just in case."*

Some people plan their weddings. Others? Their living funerals.

Each celebration is different—joyful, sacred, hilarious, tearful, or all of the above, but the common thread? They're full of life. Some are joyful. Some are funny. Some are reverent. Most are all of the above.

But here's what they're not: They're *not* about giving up. They're not about pretending death isn't coming. They're *not* a final performance. They are about *showing up* fully for life, even at the end. They're about letting love have the last word.

If you've ever thought: *"I wish I could be there to hear what people will say about me..."* Let me be the one to tell you: You can.

So, What Is a Living Funeral, Exactly?

Think of it as a **reverse memorial service**—but with you in the front row, not in a casket. A Living Funeral, also known as a *pre-funeral, life celebration,* or *end-of-life gathering,* is one of the most courageous, creative, and connective choices a person can make. It says: "I'm still here. I'm still me. And I want to leave this life awake, aware, and appreciated."

It's a time for:
- **Reflection** – Who have you been? What have you learned? What matters most?
- **Connection** – Who do you need to thank, forgive, or simply hug one more time?

- **Celebration** – What parts of your story deserve to be lifted up, laughed at, and lovingly remembered?

It's not about perfection. It's about *presence*. It's about honoring your whole life—messy bits, magic moments, and everything in between.

Why Do People Choose Living Funerals?
Here are just a few reasons:
- To hear and receive the love while they're still alive.
- To leave on their own terms—with intention and dignity.
- To say goodbye with courage, clarity, and connection.
- To model vulnerability and show others how to live—and die—well.
- To remove the mystery or fear for family and friends.
- To repair and release relationships with grace.
- To bring meaning to the moment instead of waiting for the aftermath.

What a Living Funeral Is Not
- It's not a pity party.
- It's not a premature death sentence.
- It's not a substitute for medical care, hospice, or hope.

It's a *supplement* to all of those. A sacred YES in the middle of a painful NO. A declaration that love, laughter, and legacy don't have to wait for a eulogy.

Who Should Have One?
- Anyone who wants to be celebrated while they're still alive.
- Anyone facing a terminal diagnosis.
- Anyone who wants to shape their own farewell.
- Anyone who's curious, brave, or ready.

You don't need a perfect prognosis. You just need a willing heart.

What Does a Living Funeral Look Like?
It could be in your living room. Or your backyard. Or on Zoom with friends across the globe. It can include:
- Storytelling
- Letters of gratitude
- Songs and sacred rituals
- Laughter and dancing
- Favorite foods and photo boards
- Prayers, poetry, or playlists
- Silent moments. Loud cheers. Final words.

There are no rules—just love.

What Happens After?
Sometimes, people live for days. Sometimes, for months. Sometimes, for years. But always, they live *differently*. Something shifts. In them. In us.

Because once you've been present at your own farewell, you realize something profound: You were never just passing through. You *mattered*. You belonged. And you *were loved*, not for how you died, but for how you lived.

Would *You* Consider One?
Maybe you're not ready today. Maybe this chapter just planted a seed. But one day, when the time is right, I hope you remember Ron. I hope you remember Bob. I hope you remember *yourself*. Because dying well isn't about waiting. It's about living fully—now.

And sometimes, that starts with giving yourself the honor of being celebrated out loud, while your heart is still beating, your smile still flickers, and your story still has a few lines left to write.

 **LENNY'S WHEELCHAIR WISDOM:**
Pre-funeral? Please. I call it a legacy launch party. Cake optional, but recommended. — Lenny T. Lizard

KIM HARMS
Writing Your Obituary

Why? Because it forces us to think deeply about how we want to be remembered, the values we want to embody, and the legacy we wish to leave behind.
–Brittany Drozd

Obituaries are typically written by a family member or other loved one after we die. It is another obligation we leave for our survivors, which (if they are grieving our loss) can be very difficult. It is hard to think or write clearly when we are suffering.

Why not relieve our survivors of that burden and write an obituary for ourselves, or at least an addendum to the basic obituary format of name, age of death, residence, predeceased, survivors, life summary, and funeral details? You can write your traditional obituary with just the facts or, perhaps, with some elaborations. If you believe you will be going to a "better place," you can even write a humorous and loving letter from the beyond.

My friend, Sheryl Ramstad, shared this obituary addendum (which followed the fact-sharing information part of the obituary) of an attorney friend, Don Weise. I didn't know Don, but after reading this, I hope to meet him in the afterlife. You've got to love this guy! Bravo, Don!

Workbook

"And Then"

Well, it's over. The end was not so bad and although I can now feel a pull to get on with it here, I can peek in on the funeral before I catch the train for what I think is a ballgame. Nice rainy day down there, not too warm. Not quite the crowd I expected, but then I was pretty old when I finally checked out. All the grandchildren made it, busy as they are. The children and spouses are taking it a bit harder than I wish they would, but they will be okay. And there is Shirley. This is hard for her. When you are an item for five years and then married for way over sixty years, it is hard for one to see down any road that does not include the other. But time will help, and soon we will be together again. The music was great, and no eulogies, thank God. The minister gave the straightforward Christian message, but if they really knew me, it would have been titled "Expectancies Exceeded, Possibilities Virtually Untouched." Lunch was the classic Jell-o® and potato salads, cookies and coffee, short.

As I watch this event, something (I don't seem to be totally in control here) is forcing me to think back over my life: all that has happened, all the people I have met, and all the periods of my life, whether I want to remember or not. I am told about the terrible weather on the 2 of February 1929, the day I was born, when Dad had to shovel all the way from the farmhouse to the main road to get the doctor in; and I remember the cold and heat and the amount of snow that had to be shoveled in the 1930s. I remember the peanut butter sandwiches we had to keep in the cloakroom of the country school lest they freeze solid before our noon lunchtime. I remember high school in LeSueur, my brother going to the Second World War, and my mother and father worrying as they continued to work hard. I remember hunting along the line fence with my best friend. I remember when Shirley and I got together when we were barely seventeen and her putting up with me the rest of the way. I remember attending the University of Minnesota Law School and the subsequent law practice, the work with the Golden Valley school board, the work with the Bar Association, and our house in Golden Valley. I remember all the games as player, coach, and fan, from the LeSueur Farmers to the last grandchild's last game I got to watch. I remember the slow-down years, dodging the bullet for as long as we did, learning how to live with some physical limitations, both Shirley's and mine. I remember the satisfaction I got from watching our children and their spouses and our grandchildren grow up and the unmitigated blessing they always were.

Finally, I remember with grateful appreciation all the people with whom we had the good fortune to live, the things large and small that helped us along the way, and for the good luck and proper direction we received. I have the feeling it is time to go. Someone is waiting for me. Perhaps this is when I find out whether all those hours sitting in the church pew are going to pay off. I have a good feeling about it. I saw Jesus warming up his arms a few minutes ago and he said it felt good. After all, if Jesus is pitching for me, what do I really have to worry about? Here comes the train, see you soon. Best regards and thanks for everything,

Don Wiese

It is clear from reading this that Don loved his family. He used his sense of humor to help soften the grief and remind them that he was okay. Don, you are a role model for me, and I will definitely include an obituary addendum in my legacy folder.

Here is an outline for a fun auto-obituary with an addendum. You can choose to write one or both, or neither!

Workbook

Obituary:
Name
Age
Date of death (with details if appropriate)
Where you lived
Family members that predeceased you
Family members that survived you
Life summary

Expressions of your love Funeral details

Addendum:
Greetings to those left behind

A description of the "better place" you believe you are now.

(If you think you may end up in a place that is not "better" than the earth, maybe an auto-obituary is not for you; you don't want to make the grieving worse.)

Fun memories of your life on Earth honoring your loved ones

A loving good-bye Sign off.

To download the worksheets, visit:
www.YoureNotDeadYet.Life/LegacyWorksheets

KIM HARMS

Selecting Your Obituary and Memorial Service (Funeral) Pictures

I chose my own obituary photo so I could die knowing I still had cheekbones.
—Unknown

We all want to look good when we are the center of attention, and when will you ever be more the center of attention than at your funeral? I remember that when Jim died, we scoured the pictures of him for hours to find the one we thought represented him best. My daughters and nieces created a beautiful video to play at his service, which took hours to develop.

Why not develop your own video, which you could narrate for astonishing effect, and take that pressure off your loved ones? They can always add to your creation if they find it comforting.

I also have a funeral poster already made with a background featuring the heavenly gates. I physically cut and pasted a picture of Jim, Eric, and I standing in front of the gates with the caption, "Sending you all our love, always, from our heavenly home." I would have included my mother in the group, but I did not have a picture of her that would work. I hope this picture generates some smiles.

What photograph will be selected to represent you as an obituary picture? I have already chosen mine. Jim's sense of adventure inspired it. I had the fantastic opportunity to attend the Eagle Festival in Mongolia with The Delegation for Friendship Among Women. While there, I had the chance to pose on horseback while holding an eagle spreading his wings. I had no makeup, my hair was messy, and the photograph did not capture my good side. I love it!

My children may have chosen a professional headshot with the proper lighting and my hair and makeup just right. But that is not how I want them to remember me. I want to be remembered as "Adventure Grandma." I don't know what the future will bring, and it may hold a time when I am weak, infirm, and with little memory, but at least at my funeral, my grandkids will remember that their Nana once sat on a horse, holding an eagle in the mountains surrounding the Gobi Desert! Do you have a favorite obituary picture? If not, go create one!

Ok, Kim, you've challenged me to come up with one. Here's my obituary picture from the Dead Sea!

KIM HARMS
Where Will My Remains Remain?

Whether I'm ashes in an urn, bling on a ring, roots in a tree, or abstract modern art—at least I got to choose my final act!
—Anonymous

When I was young, the only type of burial I was familiar with was a traditional burial where the body was embalmed; we had a viewing and then burial in a local cemetery. The first crematories were built in Europe and the United States in the late 1800s, but numerous cultures have been burning dead bodies since the Stone Age.

Today, there are even more options:

Traditional burial (religious or humanist) has changed over time. Years ago, the family typically took care of the body and frequently buried it in a simple wooden coffin in a local or family cemetery. More recently, funeral directors manage the care of the body and memorial services. I have to say that I appreciated this care by the White Family Funeral Homes for my son's burial and my husband's cremation. Eric was buried, and Jim's cremated remains are buried at Ft. Snelling National Cemetery. I plan to have my cremated remains buried in the same spot.

A special workshop in Ghana makes colorful works of art as coffins. Patrons of the workshop bury their dead in fanciful coffins shaped like fish, animals, pencils, or other objects that represent something important to the deceased.

Mausoleums are above-ground structures designed to hold a casket in the place of burial underground. Columbariums are above-ground structures designed to hold cremation urns.

Cremation is growing in popularity. Cremated remains can be buried or spread out in certain areas. After Eric died, I met with a remarkable group of women who had lost their children to suicide. One of the Eric Harms Libraries is dedicated to the memory of all of our sons. The ashes of three of the boys nurture a beautiful hibiscus tree and a mountainside near the library. Hindu funerals include a cremation ceremony followed by a ceremony to help the deceased's spirit enter the next world.

Burial at sea involves the disposal of the deceased into the ocean either by ship or aircraft. Cremated remains can also be disposed of in this way. Another type of burial at sea involves using the deceased's ashes to form an artificial reef by mixing the ashes with concrete before dropping the block into the ocean.

Natural or green burial is defined by the Green Burial Council as "a way of caring for the dead with the minimal environmental impact that aids in the conservation of natural resources, (and strives for) reduction of carbon emissions, protection of worker health, and the restoration or preservation of habitat. Green burial uses all biodegradable materials and does not involve embalming. A number of guidelines must be followed for a natural burial. If you are interested, check with individual state law and look for natural burial grounds, cemeteries, or preserves in your area.

Composted burial involves putting the body in a container and mixing it with straw and other organic materials to compost it. The process typically takes about thirty days. Make sure you are working with a funeral service that is fully licensed for composting and that composting bodies are a legal alternative in your state.

Diamond burials are also on the rise. Our bodies and diamonds are both made from carbon. Diamond burials involve taking the carbon from our bodies and hair and subjecting it to extremely high pressure and temperature, and then, *voila*, we are a diamond. Make sure you do your homework, select a reputable company, and follow all state laws.

Cryonics is the freezing and storage of human bodies. Many hope that the bodies can be unfrozen at a time the disease they died from has a cure. As far as I know, no human bodies have been unfrozen and revived yet.

Aquamation uses water and alkalinity to break down the body. It is then returned to the family as ash. Aquamation is considered eco-friendly as it uses significantly less energy than cremation.

Donating your body to science is one way to help humanity after you die. Donated bodies are used to train medical personnel and assist in research. It is also a donation, which means free! Make sure you use a reputable company. Many good ones are associated with a university or teaching hospital.

Space burial (or really the spreading of a memorial portion of your cremated remains) is now possible. A number of companies offer this unique service. You can have your remains shot into space, orbit the earth, and return as a "shooting star," land on the moon, or travel into the depths of the Milky Way.

Memorial art takes your cremated remains and works them into an artwork either directly or provides a special place in the artwork for the ashes.

Sky burial is typically illegal in the United States but practiced in some areas, including Tibet and Mongolia. With this practice, bodies are left on a mountaintop or hillside to decompose or be eaten by scavengers.

Whether it's dust to dust, dazzle to diamond, or roots to rebirth, don't leave your final curtain call to chance.

KIM HARMS
What Do You Want on Your Tombstone?

I lived a good life. Now I'll have a good rest.
—John Winthrop

When someone dies, especially if they die suddenly, it may be hard to find the right words to memorialize them on their headstone. When Eric died, we were so overcome with grief that all we could come up with was Beloved Son and Beloved Brother. We were better prepared when Jim passed away, and since he was cremated, we had more time before the actual burial at Ft. Snelling. We used our favorite Jim quote: "Life is an adventure!"

Writing your epitaph may serve as a tribute to you from your loved ones, and it may be appropriate to allow them to write it. However, if you want to save them the trouble, make sure you leave specific instructions in your legacy binder. Epitaphs typically include:

- Your full name
- Birth and death dates (death date to be filled out later)
- A phrase or two that will represent you to those viewing your headstone.

Also, check to ensure the epitaph is acceptable for the cemetery you choose. There may be some limitations as to what is appropriate at specific sites, and you don't want to put any additional stress on your survivors if your wishes cannot be honored or, worse yet, you have the additional expense of re-preparing the headstone.

Years ago, I was at a school board retreat, and we were asked to write our epitaph. I wrote, "She may be gone, but her fillings live on!" (This refers to my job as a dentist.) Recently a friend and fellow dentist, Dr. Michael

O'Brien, shared his epitaph with me. "Dr. Michael O'Brien: in the Largest Cavity He Has Ever Filled." We, dentists, have a good sense of humor!

Although some epitaphs will reflect the person's profession, especially if that person is a poet, writer, or musician, most will reflect a deeper part of the person's character. Some are witty, some are funny, and some reflect the loss experienced by those who loved them. Here are some of my favorites:

Martin Luther King Jr.: *"Free at Last, Free at Last, Thank God Almighty I'm Free at Last."*

Coretta Scott King: *"And now abide Faith, Hope, Love, These Three: But the greatest of these is Love. I Cor. 13:13."*

Winston Churchill: (Churchill wrote this himself fifteen years before he died.) *"I am ready to meet my Maker. Whether my Maker is prepared for the great ordeal of meeting me is another matter."*

George Burns and Gracie Allen were one of the finest comedy duos in history. They were also deeply in love. Their tomb-stone reads: *"Together Again."*

Lester Moore (Wells Fargo clerk shot down in the wild west): *"HERE LIES LESTER MOORE, FOUR SLUGS FROM A .44, NO LES NO MORE."*

If you choose to have a memorial headstone, what would you like it to say? As we age, our preferences may change. At this time, I would like to share an epitaph with Coretta Scott King. I believe passages from the Bible are fair game!

What do you want on your tombstone?

KIM HARMS

Funeral Planning: Acknowledging Your Appointment with Death

> *"None of us likes talking about death. Or funerals. But at some point, you're going to shuffle off this mortal coil and need a funeral. You can make things easier on your family and get the send-off you want by planning your own."*
> —AARP

Do you want a funeral? If the answer is no, make sure you have expressed that in writing and hopefully have discussed this with your survivors. Ensure your executor is given clear direction on making your wishes known. If you want a funeral, discuss the arrangements with your family and document your wishes. It is hard to plan anything while in the throes of grief.

- ___ Who do you feel would best honor your wishes when it's time to say goodbye?
- ___ Where would you like your funeral to be held?
- ___ Pick out your memorial/obituary photo.
- ___ Write your obituary or give information to someone else to write it.
- ___ Do you want your death to be announced on social media?
- ___ Who do you want to be contacted after you die?
- ___ Do you have an email or phone list of people you would like to notify?
- ___ Express your view on viewings.
- ___ Make sure you designate the person in charge of your funeral in writing.
- ___ What is going to happen to your body after you die? Burial, cremation, donation, etc.!
- ___ What is your funeral budget?
- ___ Have you talked with your loved ones to determine how you will be buried

___ Special Music
___ Picture board and DVD
___ Would you like to make a personal "good-bye" video?
___ Have you told your life story to ensure all the details are correct?
   A life video or story written in advance will help get the facts right.
___ Who would you like to officiate the service?
___ Religious preferences?
___ Would you like a virtual or hybrid event?

Writing your own funeral is a final love letter to those you leave behind. It's your chance to shape the story, set the tone, and make sure they remember you not just with tears, but with laughter, music, and meaning.

To download the worksheets, visit:
www.YoureNotDeadYet.Life/LegacyWorksheets

Workbook

KIM HARMS
Documenting Your Family History

"To forget one's ancestors is to be a book without a source, a tree without a root."
—Chinese proverb

Several months before my husband died, our daughter, Ashley, recorded his history in a video to submit to a company that would make the recording into a book. Unfortunately, that company went out of business. Fortunately for us, Ashley saved a copy of the video, transcribed it herself, tracked down several old pictures, and made her own book using a conventional, Internet printing service. It is a masterful display of love and a priceless family treasure.

My friend, Kim Miles, who lost two sons, showed me a book made by her son David's coworkers. David died suddenly of an aneurysm, a shock to all. His work team made a memory book filled with pictures taken over the years of his life at work. It was made digitally and then published into a book by an online printing company. What a thoughtful and comforting gift!

When our son Eric died the students at Columbia University made several books for our family. They remain valued family treasures.

We also have a video of Jim's mother, Inez, discussing her childhood in the Saskatchewan prairie. In it, she describes riding in a sled to the small village schoolhouse with hot potatoes in her pockets to keep her hands warm and, later, to eat for lunch. She describes eloping in the next town with Jim's father, Sam, during the Depression. A few years later, she bemoaned the fact that she had not yet had a child to her sisters. They recommended that Inez take a bottle of Lydia Pinkham's Elixir with "A baby in every bottle" proudly proclaimed on its label. In the next seventeen years, Inez had fourteen children. By the time Jim, number twelve, was born, the family had run out of names. The Harms children were delivered at home, and the older brothers and sisters had been lined up on the steps awaiting the first cry of their new sibling. Apparently, after a discussion on the stairwell, Jim was at least partially named after a boy one of his sisters had a crush on.

It is interesting to note that it is not always the major life accomplishments but the everyday stories we find the most interesting. Don't worry if you haven't won a Pulitzer Prize or been nominated for an Academy Award; the simple things are the most interesting when measuring your life and telling your story. If you have some funny stories about decisions you made in life, tell those. Also, stories of hardship help your survivors understand who you are and the circumstances that shaped you. Talk about how you met the people you love, about your parents, and about important lessons you learned. If you have a family history that has not been documented, this is a good time to tell the story. This is also a good time to discuss your religious and personal philosophy and your hopes for the future.

Jim's sister, Sonja, would send a "family tree" composition to all the nieces and nephews when they graduated from high school. It would include pictures of their great-grandparents, grandparents, parents, and the graduate pictured as the trunk. With commercial genealogical services, making a family tree is easier than ever and can open up a number of discussions. If possible, sharing the family's medical history can also be valuable to future generations and shared with their healthcare team.

You can start early! When each of my children graduated from high school, they got a scrapbook carefully made of printed photographs and festooned with ribbons, cut-outs, stickers, and stamps. It took me many hours to assemble each page, but my children knew that these memories were precious to me, and each book was a labor of love from their mother. For my legacy project, I am assembling a small "Adventures with NaNa" booklet for each of my grandchildren. They

Workbook

are filled with affirming thoughts and pictures of various escapades we share. Of course, as I work to construct these pages, I am motivated to seek out even more adventures! Depending on how old I get, I may need to make more adventure books!

Transferring old family videos into digital form is another way to share family history. There are many companies available that will do this for you. Some will even work with you to develop a composite video that can be shown at family gatherings or used for a memorial service. The day before Jim died, his brother showed us all a fifty-year-old video of the brothers climbing Mt Whitney. Not only did Jim enjoy looking back on his youth, but his children were also able to see what an adventurer their dad was. The miracle of digitalization allows your memories to be shared with family and friends worldwide with just a touch on your phone and can be very comforting, especially during times of loss.

You can even make a funny family video. At a recent family wedding my niece Becky commented that her Aunties resembled those in a popular commercial. This prompted us to make our own short video *Invasion of the Norwegian Aunties* that we put on YouTube. It was a family hit and memorialized a moment in time when we elderly aunties could laugh at our idiosyncrasies.

However you plan to share your legacy, the best time to start is now!

Remember, **You're Not Dead Yet!**

The first thing to do is to make a plan. The following questionnaire is designed to help you decide what is important to you, what you want to share, how you want to share, and who you want to share it with! Don't forget—you can grab these pages at YoureNotDeadYet.life and tuck them into your legal binder!

Legacy Questionnaire: Organizing Your Thoughts

Name: _____

Please describe the important people in your life who have passed away:
_____
_____
_____

What could they have said or done before they died that would have made your grief journey after they died a bit easier?
_____
_____
_____

Who are the people you expect to survive you? (Please include any loved one alive; you never know who will go first!)
_____
_____
_____

What can you share with them to let them know they are loved and help them with their grief journey?
_____
_____
_____

Do you have any examples (can be expressed anonymously) where a family member or friend failed to work out a plan for their family's financial or emotional survival? What were the consequences?
_____
_____
_____

Workbook

What do you believe will happen to you when you die? Are there some encouraging images that you can describe for your family?
_____
_____
_____

Do you have any unusual stories surrounding the death of a family member or friend?
_____
_____
_____

What goals would you like to accomplish before you die (your bucket list)? How many of these goals involve showing the important people in your life how much you love them?
_____
_____
_____

Do you have any fears about your future? Do you fear death?
_____
_____
_____

Who would benefit from a legacy letter written by you to be given to them after you pass away?
_____
_____
_____

Name them:
_____
_____
_____

You're Not Dead Yet!

Do you need to apologize to anyone? Name them:
_____
_____
_____

Who are the people in your life that made a positive difference? Would they benefit by hearing from you how grateful you are? Name them:
_____
_____
_____

From your list above, which five names would you consider the most important?
_____
_____
_____

How many letters can I get done today? _____
GET STARTED. THE SOONER, THE BETTER!

To download the worksheets, visit:
www.YoureNotDeadYet.Life/LegacyWorksheets

KIM HARMS

Legacy Letters and Legacy Love Letters:

> *If I knew words enough, I could write the longest love letter in the world and never get tired.*
> – F. Scott Fitzgerald

One of the simplest ways of sharing your legacy is to write a letter. A legacy letter, like a legacy video or book, is used to tell your story and your family's story. A legacy love letter tells your survivors how much you love or care about them and any wisdom you would like to pass along. There are no rules to writing these letters, but I will share some ideas to help you get started.

One of the oldest legacy love letters I know of was written by St. Valentine. Legend has it that he wrote to a young girl, Julia, whom he had cured of blindness. In the letter, St. Valentine encouraged her and let her know he would always be with her and would be present in her heart forever. This legacy love letter was his last act before being brought to his execution under Roman Emperor Claudius II. Julia must have appreciated the gesture, as legend also has it that she planted a beautiful almond tree above Valentine's grave.

You may want to write one legacy letter/video/book for your entire family and then personal legacy love letters for each family member.

As you write your legacy letters, keep them positive by thinking of the good they will do. This is not the time to be critical or to bring up past grievances. Write with love and the hope that what you say will be of great benefit to the recipient of the letter. Jeremy Brown writes in his book, *The Necessity of Legacy: Why Your Story Is Needed and How to Make It Last*, "Family legacy gives us confidence. Their words give us direction, comfort, and clarity. Sometimes, we just need to know the words. We need to hear them, and we need to feel them."

You're Not Dead Yet!

"We are simply asking our patriarchs and matriarchs to be bold in their declarations. To be honest in their storytelling and to speak loving words to the generations that will proceed with them. Because their legacy is a priceless gift. Their memories, their beliefs, their values, and their history mean everything for all of us in years to come... Legacy gives us affirmation, and it matters."

One of my closest friends described a letter written to her son when he was born. It was from her father. She wants to remain anonymous, so we will just use the first names here. It was meant to be opened when her son was eighteen years old.

> *My Dear, Dear John,*
>
> *You were born two days ago.*
>
> *I called your father and felt so completely happy that you had come into this world. I also felt so proud of your mother... and how she has handled your pregnancy. I had gone to mass at St. Francis Chapel on the ground floor of the Prudential Building [in Boston]. My prayer that day was for you and your mother. The next day I went again.*
>
> *I know your brother Joe wanted a brother. When we visited... at Easter, Joe had a new outfit of clothes, and he said he wanted to dress like a big brother.*
>
> *I called Grandma Ellen tonight. She said you were (are) beautiful. Joe and Larry were getting a new baseball uniform and having a picture taken.*
>
> *So, John, I'm thrilled you are here. I will be working to see you have a decent world to inhabit if we have not solved poverty, pollution, torture, racism, and hate, and if there ain't enough love, to do something about it.*
>
> *I love you, Grandpa John.*

I love this letter. Grandpa John wrote a letter to welcome his grandson at birth, and Don Weise wrote a letter (obituary) to say goodbye! What kind of letter can you create for those you love? available for download at You'reNotDeadYet.Life/legacy.

Sample Template for Legacy Love Letter

Dear _____,

I am so grateful (blessed, thankful, happy) to have had you in my life. (Then describe why and extoll their good virtues.)

When I look back on our (my) family, the most important things I learned were _____. My Faith has taught me _____. What matters most to me is _____. My hope for you is _____.

Thank you again for all that you brought into my life. With all my love,

Mom (Grandma, Dad, Grandpa, Name)

Optional Script on the Tasks of Mourning

Please adjust and adapt as you see fit and customize it. The intent is to bring comfort.

My dear _____,

Psychologist J. William Worden described four tasks that help us understand how we journey through grief. He described them as the Four Tasks of Mourning. Everyone proceeds through these tasks in different ways and at different times. Everyone's journey is unique. I hope that your voyage through these tasks is short and that you will remember me with happiness in your heart, not sadness.

Task Number One: Accept the Reality of the Loss
When I am gone, it may take some time to realize that (describe something that you do on a regular basis), I am not physically present to participate in the things we shared. (Describe holidays, events, or favorite subjects you had in common.) Although I am no longer there in the flesh, please know that my spirit and love will always be with you.

Task Number Two: Process the Pain
I believe this is typically the hardest task. Grief is painful. The brain processes it as a traumatic experience. Processing that pain may take weeks or months or years. Everyone manages differently. Please work hard on this task and fight through the grief as hard as possible. You may feel sometimes that you have conquered it, but a date on the calendar, a memory, or an event can strike you right back down again. If it does, battle again to get back up!

Task Number Three: Adjust to Your New World
When someone dies, your own identity changes in that you no longer have that relationship in a physical sense. I hope I have prepared you well for a time without me, but please strive to adapt to the void I leave. You may need to learn to (manage the finances, take out the trash, or teach the grandkids how to fish). Please know and understand that you are enough even if you are alone.

Task Number Four: Find a New Life with an Enduring Connection
I want you to be happy, and the best way you can honor my life is to live yours with happiness and joy. One of my main missions in life is to help my loved ones become kind, caring, compassionate, and joyful people, no matter what their circumstances. Your joy brings honor to my life. Work for it.

With much (love, affection, respect etc.)

(Your name in familiar, loving terms, Mom, Dad, Grandpa……)

Template for Letter to be Given at Important Events:

The most important part of this type of letter is to be loving and sincere. Use personal anecdotes whenever possible! Keep it unique to your relationship!

>Dear _____,
>Congratulations on this special day. (Specify graduation, wedding, birthday.)
>
>I am so proud of you. (Specify again.)
>
>I remember when_____.
>
>My hope for you is _____.
>
>The best advice I can give you is_____. Please know how much I love you!
>
>Mom, Dad, Grandma, or Grandpa

Words of Wisdom and Legacy Questions for Legacy Letters and Love Letters:

___ Important things you learned in your life and people who mattered
___ Special words for each person
___ What makes them unique?
___ Special advice for their future your hopes for them
___ Faith
___ Failure
___ Success
___ Education
___ What can they learn from historical conflicts?
___ Raising a family
___ Cultural lessons

___ Favorite moments to cherish and promote in the future vacation
___ Family
___ Work
___ Lessons for raising a family
___ Special talents or hobbies
___ General advice.

To download the worksheets, visit:
www.YoureNotDeadYet.Life/LegacyWorksheets

Reconciliation Letters

Reconciliation and forgiveness can actually help all of us move on in a healthier, happier way.
—Chesa Boudin

Is there someone important in your life that you are estranged from and whose relationship you miss? Is that person deserving of a second chance? Would contacting that person be a healthy choice for you? If so, perhaps you should consider a reconciliation letter.

Reconciliation (according to the Oxford dictionary) is the restoration of friendly relations. Forgiveness and grace are necessary to reconcile.

There is no need to establish who was right and wrong, even if you feel right. If you were wrong, then an apology would be a good way to start a reconciliation. You are the one initiating an attempt to reconcile, and the best way to do that is to show grace to the other person.

As a Christian, I believe that Jesus died on the cross to reconcile me with God, and therefore, I must do my part to reconcile with my brothers and sisters (that means everybody) here on Earth.

Other religions also teach the importance of reconciliation, and even those who do not profess religious beliefs understand the importance of working toward harmony among their fellow humans.

The difference between a reconciliation letter and an apology letter is that a reconciliation letter does not have to admit blame. Neither letter should assign blame to anyone else. A reconciliation letter should focus on rebuilding the relationship. The goal is harmony.

So, what are the steps to reconcile? The first step is ensuring you are adequately motivated to seek reconciliation. The best motivator is love (romantic, brotherly, or unconditional). If you love the other person, you would be willing to make some sacrifices to reconcile. Look inward to understand your responsibility for the separation. Forgive the other person's role. Show empathy, compassion, and remorse for your role in the disagreement. Then reach out, in love, to do the restoration work.

I understand that there are many people who have been hurt to such a degree that attempting to reconcile, especially if the other person does not express remorse, would cause them even more pain. Some individuals would take advantage of the opportunity of a repaired relationship and create additional suffering. In other cases, a repaired relationship might not be appropriate or open a new can of worms. Use your judgment and your heart to make the decision when deciding to reconcile. You can still free your heart through forgiveness without bringing the other person back into your life.

Reconciliation Letter Template

Dear____,

I miss you (expound upon why you miss them) _____
_____ . Over the last (weeks, months, years), I have learned _____
_____ . Our relationship is more important than any disagreement between us.

Can we meet for (coffee, tea, dinner, lunch, phone call)? With (warm regards, best wishes, love)

Your name (informal name)

Reconciliation Letter Tips

- Start by telling the person how much you value your relationship. Express your gratitude for having this person in your life.
- No need to blame anyone but express your remorse over your part in the disagreement if appropriate. You don't have to be in the wrong to reconcile; remember, the goal is to build a harmonious relationship. Keep your tone gracious and humble. Oversee your words, and don't include hidden agendas or trigger comments.
- Look for a solution, such as avoiding a topic that causes dissent. Agree to disagree.
- Restate your desire to heal the relationship and how much you value the person.

Reconciliation Quotes for Inspiration:

Reconciliation is more beautiful than victory.
—Violeta Chamorro

It is much safer to reconcile an enemy than to conquer him; victory may deprive him of his poison, but reconciliation of his will.
—Owen Feltham

Reconciliation is a decision that you take in your heart.
—Ingrid Betancourt

A word of truth can mobilize two people looking for the road to reconciliation.
—Donald Trusk

KIM HARMS
Apology Letters

Apologizing does not always mean you're wrong and the other person is right. It just means you value your relationship more than your ego.
—Mark Matthews

None of us are perfect, and we all make mistakes. Unfortunately, at least in the US, I believe that we are addicted to being right, and we are too frequently offended. Both of these attributes can lead to problems and can lead us to do things that hurt others. Giving grace and forgiveness to others is a beautiful gift that can free us from our negative feelings. One of my dear friends in Rwanda told me that forgiveness is like the metamorphosis of a butterfly. You start out with anger or resentment that resembles the characteristics of an ugly caterpillar always eating things up. Through the process of forgiveness, you change into a beautiful butterfly free of the earth and able to fly to the heavens. The people in Rwanda know about forgiveness!

One of the most important things we can teach our children is to understand that they are sometimes wrong, and it is essential to recognize when they are wrong and make things right.

The first step in making things right is to apologize. The best time to apologize is immediately and in person. If that chance passes you by and you are uncomfortable talking about the situation, a written apology will do the trick. Understand that an apology doesn't guarantee forgiveness, but it surely increases the chances, and you will have the peace of knowing that you have done your part.

Written apologies are particularly helpful if the situation is very emotional or if the person you are apologizing to is so hurt that they may respond uncomfortably. Written apologies can be in email form, but the most personal is a letter, preferably hand-written (if you have legible handwriting).

As a quick review: According to *Psychology Today*, there are three parts to an effective apology: acknowledgment, remorse and empathy, and restitution.

To express remorse, you might say that you regret what happened or wish for another outcome. If you feel you did something wrong, you might say you are sorry for your actions. Expressing sadness at the loss of the relationship is another way to express remorse.

Empathy means that you put yourself in the shoes of the other person. One of the best ways to express empathy is to openly listen or think carefully about how the other person must feel and validate those feelings. Using words like, "You must feel so (unhappy, betrayed, sad, angry)" will help the other person understand that you care about them.

Restitution means to give back or restore. If there is something you can do to right the wrong, do it! Sometimes, especially when your words hurt someone else, letting them know that you are sorry you let those words out and that you did not mean them is all you can do. Need help getting your apology letter started? Here are some tips and words that may be useful!

First of all, let go of your ego. Make sure your tone is respectful, courteous, and thoughtful; humility is the key. Show your love for this person as a fellow human being.

Make sure all the apology parts are included:
- Acknowledgment
- Admit your mistake, simply, with no excuses.
- Remorse and empathy
- Describe how you may have made that person feel.
- Describe how the realization that you caused him or her pain made you feel.

- What have you learned? Why you won't do this again.
- Restitution
- What you will do to make things better and show your remorse.
- Ask for forgiveness
- Asking for forgiveness is important. Forgive them for any part they may have played, but don't mention this in the letter unless they have asked for forgiveness, as telling them you forgive them weakens your apology to them by highlighting the wrongs they committed.
- Realize that the other person may not forgive you. Knowing that you are offering a sincere apology and doing what you can to make things right should give you some peace. You can't control the behavior of others. Apologizing, like forgiveness, can set you free.

Apology letter template

Dear_____,

I am so sorry that I (no excuses, you are just sorry)_____
_____

You must have felt (or I can't imagine how you felt) _____
_____

I feel _____
_____

I know now that _____
_____

I will never do this again _____
_____.

Can you forgive me?

With (warm regards, love, gratitude) Your name (informal)

Apology Quotes for Inspiration

"Never forget the nine most important words of any family-I love you. You are beautiful. Please forgive me."

— H. Jackson Brown Jr.

"Chocolate says 'I'm sorry' so much better than words."

—Rachel Vincent, My Soul to Save (Works for me!)

Don't wait for the perfect words—start the conversation, and let grace fill in the gaps.

— Kim Harms

Live Well. Die Well. Reflect Deeply.

1. To me, living well today means...

2. If I treated myself like someone I deeply cared about, I would...

3. The one thing I need to shed now is...

4. If I had one year to live, I would...

5. I feel most alive when I...

6. The most life-giving habit I could start today is...

7. One small step I can take today toward living well is...

8. The story I'm ready to stop telling myself is...

9. The thing I've been avoiding that matters most is...

10. The most loving thing I can do for myself right now is...

11. One boundary I need to set to protect my peace is...

12. The most important characteristic I want to be remembered for...

13. If I truly honored my body, mind, and spirit, I would...

14. One relationship I want to heal before I die is...

15. I would feel more freedom if I let go of...

16. One truth about myself I need to fully embrace is...

17. If I fully lived the way I was meant to, my life would look like...

18. To care for myself well, I need to stop... and start...

19. The legacy I want to leave is...

20. What haven't I said to my family about my death that I need to talk about?

21. If you lived the same way today as you do in 5 years, what will your life look like?

22. One regret I don't want to have on my deathbed is...

23. To me, dying well means...

24. What gives me the most peace when I think about dying is...

25. The biggest fear I have about dying is...

To download the worksheets, visit:
www.YoureNotDeadYet.Life/LegacyWorksheets

About the Authors

Kimberly Harms D.D.S., GC-C
**Death Doula • Life Coach • Civil Mediator
Legacy Builder • Certified Grief Counselor**

Dr. Kimberly Harms has been around the block in life — several times. She has served as a Commissioned Officer in the United States Public Health Service, a dental school professor, a clinical dentist with her late husband Jim in Farmington MN, a school board Chair, President of an international women's organization, Vice Chair of the Union Gospel Mission Board, the first woman President of the Minnesota Dental Association, and a National Spokesperson for the American Dental Association (21 years).

After 30 years in clinical practice, Dr. Harms lost her ability to practice dentistry due to nerve damage in her "drilling fingers".

This event forced a complete change of career direction. She recalibrated. Then became a grief counselor, a civil mediator, a death doula, a life coach, an award-winning, best-selling author, and international speaker on the topics of grief, conflict, and legacy planning.

Having also experienced devastating personal losses—including the suicides of both her beautiful mother and brilliant son, followed by the death of her beloved husband from a broken heart—Kim now devotes her life to walking alongside others in pain. She leads faith-based widow support groups and coaches Baby Boomers through the rocky terrain of life's fourth quarter, guiding them toward healing, hope, meaning, and purpose. Her passion is helping others overcome heartache, change, and build a life worth living—a life of laughter, legacy, and love.

Dr. Harms honors the life of her book-loving son, Eric, who dreamed of becoming a lawyer, by co-founding 65 Eric Harms Memorial

Libraries through Books for Africa, spreading knowledge and hope across Rwanda. These libraries—found in primary schools, secondary schools, churches, universities, national institutions, medical and dental schools, and even four complete new law libraries—stand as a testament to Eric's passion for learning and love for the rule of law. In the process, she formed lifelong friendships and often says she has learned a great deal about resilience from her Rwandan friends, calling them "the best grief counselors in the world."

Dr. Harms holds many titles, but the ones closest to her heart are "Mom" to her two remarkable daughters and "Nana" to her six precious, delightful grandchildren. Splitting her time between Kansas City and Minneapolis, she embraces every opportunity to savor the laughter, love, and unforgettable moments with all six of them—because, in the end, it's family that defines her richest legacy.

Top Requested Seminars and Workshops
- Are You Ready? How to Build a Legacy to Die For
- Escape From the Valley of the Scammed
- How to Get Along With Your Adult Children Without Really Trying
- Everything You Need to Know Before You Go
- I'm Still Here: Redefining Your Purpose After the Loss of a Spouse
- Unwrapping Hope For the Holidays
- You're Not Dead Yet! (Keynote with Kathy Dempsey)
- The Clock is Ticking? Are You Ready (Keynote with Kathy Dempsey)

Awards:
- University of Rwanda First Friend Award
- Mshale Newspaper's African Founder's Award
- International College of Dentists Leadership in Journalism Award
- American Student Dental Association Advocate of Excellence Award
- American Dental Association Access to Care Award

About the Authors

- Books for Africa Kilimanjaro Society Award
- Minnesota Dental Association's Distinguished Service Award
- Pacific Book Awards Best Inspirational Book of 2024
- Independent Press Awards: Best Death and Dying book 2024
- San Francisco Book Awards Best Wildcard Book 2024
- American Writers Award: Best Death and Dying Book 2025
- Outstanding Creator Award Champion, Best Non-Fiction 2024
- Literary Global Book Award: Best Parent/Family Motivational Book 2025
- Book of Excellence: Best Death and Dying 2025

Numerous other honors, including those from Readers Choice, Chanticleer, Global, International, New York Book Festival, Hollywood Book Festival, Literary Titan, Southern California Book Festival, Penn Craft, and NYC Big Book Awards.

Author of:
- *Are You Ready? How to Build a Legacy to Die For*
- *Naomi and the Widow's Club* (with Naomi Rhode)
- *Naomi and the Widow's Club Workbook* (with Naomi Rhode)
- *Rebirth: Stories of Unyielding Courage* (contributor)
- *Emotional Emergency Handbook*
- *Neutralize Your Nightmares: Promote Office Harmony through Structured Conflict Management*
- *Tenacious Leadership*
- *Living Your Strengths: A Grievers Guide to Life After Loss*
- *Overcoming Fear and the Battle in Our Brains*
- *The Secret Life of Grief*
- *Keeping out of Harm's Way*

Email: Kim@YoureNotDeadYet.Life

Kathy B. Dempsey, RN, MEd, CSP
Keynote Speaker • Change Expert
Life Coach • Death Doula
Living Funeral Celebrant

Kathy B. Dempsey didn't expect a death sentence at 25. But when she became the first healthcare worker in the U.S. to test HIV positive—after a traumatic ER exposure—she was forced to confront something even more terrifying than illness: the realization that, even as a trauma nurse, she wasn't prepared to die. That wake-up call became her greatest teacher.

Now, as the founder of *The Shedding Revolution*™ and President of *Keep Shedding! Inc.*, Kathy empowers people to master the lifelong art of letting go—from their first breath to their final bow. A seasoned healthcare leader, she has served as Director of Nursing for Life Care Centers of America, Administrator of Psychiatric and Chemical Dependency Services, and Director of the Alzheimer's Day Care Center at Memorial Health Care System. She also led Memorial's organizational development efforts to become one of the top 100 hospitals in America.

An award-winning author of eight books, Kathy's work blends real-world wisdom with deep personal insight. Her bestselling book, *Shed or You're Dead*®: *31 Unconventional Strategies for Growth and Change*, won a Writer's Digest International Book Award. Kathy's mission has reached Fortune 500 leaders, healthcare heroes, and everyday changemakers around the world.

She is also the founder of *The Keep Shedding Educational Foundation*, a 501(c)(3) nonprofit that has helped send more than 300 AIDS orphans to school in Zambia. Surprisingly, it was the children who became her greatest teachers—finding joy in the smallest things, laughing easily,

About the Authors

and reminding her that happiness isn't about having everything... it's about shedding expectations (and maybe dancing whenever possible).

As a death doula trained at the Omega Institute and an educator with a master's degree focused on Death & Dying, Kathy brings a rare combination of wisdom, wit, and grounded compassion to every threshold moment—whether it's shedding a job, a fear, an identity, or this life itself.

Accompanied by her metaphorical sidekick, *Lenny the Lizard*, Kathy reminds us that life is one big, beautiful chance to SHED anything that keeps us from living fully. Rooted in her personal mantra, "From birth to death, we continually let go of the old and take on the new" she invites each of us to shed boldly, love deeply, and show up lighter for the journey. She now carries forward the message gifted to her by her beloved partner Ron: **"You die well by living well today."**

Kathy was born in Washington, D.C. and spent several years living in the hills of Tennessee, where she deepened her passion for psychology, spiritual growth, and helping others SHED. She now lives in Scottsdale, Arizona, with her lizard Lenny, an expert in the art of shedding, and her 7-pound Maltese, Gabriel, a breed famously known for not shedding. Go figure.

Top Requested SHED® Keynotes & Workshops:
- Shed or You're Dead®: How to Stay Alive & Thrive in the Midst of Change
- SHED® 2.0: How to Lead Change When You Don't Agree With It Yourself
- SuperSHED: Live Well. Die Well. Choose Well.
- SHED HAPPENS: 7 Ways to Overcome Challenges at Work and in Life
- Strategic Shedding Celebration: Celebrating in Advance
- Would You Ever Consider a Living Funeral?
- You're Not Dead Yet! *(with Dr. Kim Harms)*
- The Clock Keeps Ticking: Are You Ready? *(with Dr. Kim Harms)*

Accomplishments & Awards:
- Certified Speaking Professional (CSP) – Highest earned speaking designation (less than 10% worldwide)
- Voted Top 5 Speaker (two years in a row) – Speaker.com
- Writer's Digest International Book Awards – *Shed or You're Dead®* and *A Gift from a Thief*
- Top 10 Finalist – North America's Next Greatest Speaker
- Showcase Speaker of the Year – Georgia Speakers Association
- Led Memorial Health Care System's transformation into a Top 100 U.S. Hospital

Author of Eight Books + Contributions:
- *Shed or You're Dead®: 31 Unconventional Strategies for Growth & Change*
- *SHED Survival Guides* (Healthcare Professionals, Every Employee & Manager)
- *SHED HAPPENS: 7 Ways to Overcome Challenges at Work and in Life*
- *SHED Evaluation: 52 Thought-Provoking Questions* (Standard & COVID Editions)
- *Kids Survival Guide – Dealing with Hurt*
- *God is Enough: Shedding Whatever It Takes to Experience a Deeper Relationship with Self, Others, and God*
- *Naomi & The Widows Club: A Safe, Strong Place After the Loss of a Spouse*
- *A Gift from a Thief*
- Contributing author to two *Chicken Soup for the Soul* bestsellers

Clients Include:
Aetna, Allergan, Alive Hospice, American Heart Association, Bayer, Catholic Health Initiatives, Cedars-Sinai, Delta Air Lines, Disney, GE Capital, Giant Foods, Habitat for Humanity, Hearst Corp., Honeywell, Johns Hopkins, Kronos, Mayo Clinic, Meeting Planners International, National Hospice and Palliative Care Organization, Nestlé, Northeastern University, Ohio State, Penn State, Pfizer, SHRM, Texas Workforce Commission, Verizon Wireless, Wells Fargo—and many more.

Email: Kathy@YoureNotDeadYet.Life

About the Authors

Lenny T. Lizard
(middle name - The)
**Mascot • Metaphor
Mentor in a Wheelchair**

Lenny the Lizard met Kathy B. Dempsey on July 29, 1998, during a life-changing hallway conversation at Memorial Hospital in Chattanooga, Tennessee. A colleague's pet lizard had just died—because it didn't shed its skin. That odd but powerful moment sparked something unforgettable: *Shed or You're Dead*® and a lifelong metaphor was born.

Since then, Lenny has served as Kathy's alter ego, co-conspirator, and Chief Energy Officer (CEO) of *Keep Shedding! Inc.* He earned his Ph.D. in Shedding from the prestigious Reptile University and has traveled the globe—perched on heads, stirring up laughter, and inspiring transformation in boardrooms, breakrooms, and ballrooms alike.

As the years slithered on, Lenny swapped his sprint for a smooth roll. These days, he sports reading glasses, uses a wheelchair, and delivers his legendary zingers with a little more pause and a lot more wisdom.

But don't worry, Lenny's not going anywhere. He's still here, offering his signature wheelchair wisdom, reminding you (with a wink and a wisecrack) that shedding is a lifelong skill. His son, *Lenny Jr.*, is the one hitting the road more these days—full of energy, fresh perspectives, and just enough sass to make his dad proud. *Lenny the Elder* may be rolling a little slower, but he's not retiring—he's just getting wiser with every spin of the wheels. **Two tails. One mission: Keep Shedding.**

How Can We Support You?

You've made it to the final pages—but your journey is just beginning.

We care deeply about helping you *live well, die well*, and everything in between. Whether you're shedding the old, embracing the new, planning ahead, or simply curious about what comes next—we're here for you.

Let's keep the conversation going. Let us walk with you. Here's how we can continue to support you:

Our Services Include:
Speaking, Workshops & Retreats
Inspiring, interactive sessions to spark transformation and open up meaningful dialogue.

Life Transitions Coaching
Personalized support to navigate major life changes with clarity and courage.

End-of-Life Planning
Create a plan that reflects your values, wishes, and voice.

Living Funerals & Festivals of Life
Celebrate your life with intention, laughter, and love—while you're still here to enjoy it.

Legacy Projects
Capture your story, wisdom, and impact for future generations.

Life Review
Reflect on where you've been, what you've learned, and what matters most now.

Mediation & Advocacy
Support for families navigating difficult conversations, decisions, and transitions.

After-Death Care Planning & Services
Honor your final wishes with dignity and meaning.

Grief Support
Compassionate guidance for healing hearts—before and after loss.

Legacy Planning
Define how you want to be remembered and the impact you want to leave behind.

Stay Connected
Sign up for free resources, thoughtful articles, and inspiring podcast episodes at http://www.YoureNotDeadYet.life/

Have a question or want to talk with us directly? We'd love to hear from you.

Email: info@YoureNotDeadYet.Life

LENNY'S PARTING WISDOM
You don't have to have it all figured out—just keep shedding, one scale at a time. We're here when you need us. Wheels ready. Wisdom loaded. — Lenny T. Lizard

www.ingramcontent.com/pod-product-compliance
Lightning Source LLC
Chambersburg PA
CBHW070643160426
43194CB00009B/1561